ADAPTIVE CURIOSITY

ADAPTIVE CURIOSITY

How HUMANS FIND PURPOSE *in the* AGE OF INTELLIGENT MACHINES

DIANE HAMILTON, PhD

WILEY

Published by John Wiley & Sons, Inc., Hoboken, New Jersey.

For general information on our other products and services or for technical support, please contact our Customer Care Department within the United States at (800) 762-2974, outside the United States at (317) 572-3993 or fax (317) 572-4002.

Wiley also publishes its books in a variety of electronic formats. Some content that appears in print may not be available in electronic formats. For more information about Wiley products, visit our website at www.wiley.com.

Library of Congress Cataloging-in-Publication Data:

Names: Hamilton, Diane author
Title: Adaptive curiosity : how humans find purpose in the age of intelligent machines / Dr. Diane Hamilton.
Description: Hoboken, NJ : Wiley, [2027] | Includes index.
Identifiers: LCCN 2026024300 (print) | LCCN 2026024301 (ebook) | ISBN 9781394455171 hardback | ISBN 9781394455195 adobe pdf | ISBN 9781394455188 epub
Subjects: LCSH: Curiosity | Adaptability (Psychology) | Motivation (Psychology)
Classification: LCC BF323.C8 H365 2027 (print) | LCC BF323.C8 (ebook)
LC record available at https://lccn.loc.gov/2026024300
LC ebook record available at https://lccn.loc.gov/2026024301

Cover Design: Wiley
Cover Images: SKIMP Art/Adobe Stock, Aku/Adobe Stock, pixel ground/Adobe Stock - images Generated with AI.
Author Photo: Courtesy of the Author
SKY10167176_082826

For Kasen and Hayden

Contents

Introduction

Over the course of my career, I have been fortunate to have had the opportunity to interview thousands of people. One individual who left a lasting impression on me was Albert Bandura. If you never took a psychology course, his name might not immediately stand out. In his field, though, he was considered a giant. He was one of the most cited researchers in history and widely known for how much he shaped the way people understand human behavior.

I met him when he was a guest on my radio show. We developed a friendship from that experience, and later, he graciously invited my daughter and me to visit him at his home on the Stanford campus in Palo Alto.

I can still picture that warm California afternoon clearly. He sat in what was obviously his favorite chair slightly off to our left, while my daughter and I sat on an older couch diagonally across from him. We talked for hours. It was clear he enjoyed sharing what he had learned with anyone curious enough to listen.

As he spoke about his research career, you could feel his enthusiasm. He told stories about decades of studying human behavior and working with people who struggled with fear.

He explained that some fears were understandable while others were completely irrational. He described an example he had worked with many times. Some people were terrified of snakes. Certain individuals could not even hear the word. If someone said, "snake!" they might tense up, sweat, or physically pull back. Others could not look at a photograph. Even a drawing was too much for some people.

He walked me through the process he used to help people gradually become comfortable with the snake. First, he would get them to simply talk about it. He would ask what the person believed might happen if they encountered a snake. Would it jump? Would it attack? What exactly were they imagining? They would stay at that stage until the person could say the word without panic.

The next steps would slowly unfold. They might look at a photograph or stand outside the room where the snake was kept and eventually enter while keeping their distance. Bandura would calmly handle the snake while the participant would watch. When nothing dramatic happened, the person eventually felt comfortable enough to move closer and then eventually hold it.

After Bandura finished telling that story, he leaned toward us and said, "The snake is not the treatment. The belief is the treatment."

Bandura explained that this idea came directly from his research on self-efficacy. If you have not studied psychology, self-efficacy refers to your ability to succeed in specific situations. Psychologists once believed that we could change behavior mainly through rewards, punishments, or instructions. Yet Bandura's work kept pointing to something else. He found that whether or not someone persisted was influenced by whether they believed they could succeed before they even started.

He told me that when people experienced even a small success or watched someone like themselves handle a challenge, like holding a snake, something inside them shifted. Their expectations about themselves changed, and they were able to stay with a task longer. They felt more comfortable pushing themselves to do more. Over time, those small experiences began to influence what they believed they were capable of doing.

The person who eventually held the snake had not suddenly become brave. They had just gathered enough information about themselves to believe they could handle it.

Bandura explained to us that when someone experiences what he called mastery experiences, even small successes begin to build belief, and that belief leads them to persist, and that persistence leads to greater ability. If you think about it, this applies to far more than learning how to handle a snake.

Today, many people are facing a different kind of snake. It might not be something you can place in a room or point to directly like that, but technology has created a new kind of fear. You might feel a sense of something frightening coming from conversations about artificial intelligence, automation, and the uncomfortable question many are asking about where they might fit as these technologies evolve.

People are wondering whether the abilities they spent years developing will still matter in the future. The question is not whether technology can perform certain tasks faster or cheaper, because we know it can. The deeper concern is whether the years people spent learning a craft, building expertise, and developing a career could disappear overnight as machines begin doing more of that work.

A few years after we sat together in that living room, Albert Bandura passed away. His death came just before technological change began accelerating in ways few people had predicted.

Today, we live in a world of intelligent machines. Artificial intelligence, advanced software systems, and robots can simulate forms of reasoning, learning, and problem solving that once seemed uniquely human. Some research has shown they can even simulate artificial curiosity. These technologies have already started changing the future of work and will keep advancing in ways no one can fully predict.

Sometimes I find myself wondering what Bandura might say about this moment in history. How would he interpret the fear many people feel about a future where intelligent machines perform tasks that once defined entire professions? What advice might he give to someone who wonders where their sense of purpose will come from if work changes dramatically?

My guess is he would remind us that people do not find their purpose because a system assigns it to them. People discover meaning when they see that what they do actually makes a difference.

Whether the challenge you face involves a snake, a difficult task, or uncertainty about the future, it works the same way. When you face something step by step and see that you can handle it, you feel more in control.

People often assume the biggest fear about the future is technology replacing jobs. In reality, people are mostly unsettled by something deeper. Naturally, they are concerned about their work disappearing, but the root issue is identity.

How will people be able to answer if someone new they meet casually asks, what do you do?

For generations that question has revealed more about us than most people realize. The answer explains someone's competence, income, ambition, belonging, and status. It tells other people where to place you, and it tells you where you stand. The answer to what you do has become proof that your days matter.

For most of modern history, that arrangement felt stable. You learned something useful, entered a field, built routines around deadlines and responsibilities, and then measured your progress in promotions, performance reviews, and milestones. Even when work was frustrating, there was a sense of structure. There was somewhere to go and something that needed you. Now, many people sense that structure is shifting, and with that shift, people can feel as if the map they relied on for direction has faded.

Personal meaning has never come from a job alone. When people describe the moments in life that felt most significant, they rarely point to a title or a paycheck. They talk about experiences they had. They remember helping someone succeed, solving a difficult problem, discovering an idea that changed how they saw the world, or creating something that did not exist before.

When you look at those experiences more closely, you start to see a pattern. Across very different lives and circumstances, people tend to find meaning in a few common places.

Over time, I noticed four areas where people most often experience a sense of purpose. For some people, it comes from exploring ideas and learning new things. For others, it grows out of connecting with people in meaningful ways. It may come from creating something that did not exist before, or from influencing a group or community in a way that felt significant to them.

Very few people experience meaning from only one of these. Most of us draw from a mix of them. The difference is that certain areas tend to energize us more than others.

This book will help you as a reader explore those four areas and discover where your own sense of purpose is strongest. Instead of waiting for a job or an organization to define your role or what you will do with the time in your day, you will learn how to recognize the kinds of experiences that give your life meaning.

This will require you to develop adaptive curiosity, which is your ability to keep exploring even when the structures you relied on begin to change. This allows you to experiment, learn, and build confidence the same way Bandura's participants did in the snake experiment, one step at a time.

As you move through the book, you will see how these four areas can guide you toward new ways of contributing, learning, creating, and connecting in a world where work itself may look very different from what you and previous generations expected.

The rest of this book explores how you can reconnect with these sources of meaning when the traditional systems that once organized your life begin to shift. Each section examines a different part of that transition, from understanding why identity became tied to your occupation, to recognizing the barriers that prevent reinvention, to learning how you can explore, connect, create, and contribute in a world shaped by intelligent machines.

The scale of change happening today is unlike anything any of us have experienced in our lifetimes, and even the concept of identity feels less stable than it once did.

Identity is not simply a job title or a list of traits you have. It is the story you believe about who you are, what you value, where you belong, and how you contribute.

Think about how your identity has been influenced by your career. For me, I spent my career helping leaders and organizations think differently about business, engagement, and innovation. I have also spent decades teaching, speaking, and researching how people grow inside systems. When intelligent machines began advancing faster than many expected, I found myself asking a question that is becoming hard to avoid: As systems change dramatically, what happens to those of us whose identities were built inside them?

This book began as my attempt to explore that question honestly. Like many people, I had spent years building a career inside systems that provided structure, expectations, and direction. When those systems began evolving faster than anyone anticipated, I started examining some assumptions I had rarely questioned.

I knew I could not predict which technologies would dominate the future or which jobs might disappear. I was interested in something far more personal.

How do you build a life that still feels meaningful when the structure you relied on begins to change? How do you design direction for yourself when no organization determines it?

Bandura's research helped me recognize something important. The answers will not come from dramatic predictions about the future, but we can learn a lot from the same principle he used in the snake experiment: Belief develops through small, deliberate actions. Your identity strengthens as you accumulate evidence. If fear can shrink step by step, your capacity can expand step by step as well.

When a familiar structure disappears, it creates a space that can feel unsettling, yet that same space also creates an opportunity. It becomes the moment when you stop inheriting your identity from a system and begin shaping it on your own, and that can be empowering.

As you read this, you are likely experiencing some of that tension brought about by all the change happening right now.

You might feel like the ground beneath your familiar roles is shifting. You may be questioning how you can remain useful, engaged, and purposeful in a world where intelligent machines continue to advance. You are not the only one feeling that way. It helps to know that you have an opportunity to discover your purpose if no one dictates it for you.

Before he became a famous psychologist, Albert Bandura was simply a curious young man who believed he could learn what he did not yet know. Recognition and titles came later, but his belief came first. We now live in a time when your beliefs will dictate how you respond to this new world.

Intelligent machines will certainly reshape industries, automate tasks, and alter how work is organized. What they cannot replace is the human capacity to learn, contribute, and participate in ways that matter to others.

This book shares the framework I have been developing as I navigate this same moment of change with you. It grows from decades of research on curiosity, thousands of conversations with leaders and innovators, and my own effort to understand how people continue building meaningful lives when familiar structures evolve. It will help you recognize where your sense of meaning can still be created, how to move toward it without someone pushing you there, and how to build a sense of purpose even as the structures around work continue to evolve.

The rise of intelligent machines does not erase your place in the world. It changes how that place is discovered. More importantly, it gives you the opportunity to design it.

ADAPTIVE CURIOSITY

PART I

When Identity and Occupation Separate

CHAPTER 1

What Do You Do?

If you are anything like me, you probably ask the question, "What do you do?" when you meet someone new. It's one of those natural parts of a conversation, along with "Where are you from?" and "How is your day going?" If you think about it, the answer to "What do you do?" often tells us much more than we realize. In a surprisingly small number of words, people reveal their education, ambition, financial success, and sometimes even how they compare themselves to other people in the room. The question can sound casual, but most of us instinctively understand that it carries weight.

For a long time, it felt completely normal to ask it. The answer you give might reveal whether you worked outside the home, cared for children or family members, studied in school, volunteered in a community, or pursued something you cared deeply about. This question often drifts toward occupations because jobs tend to define us. If you have a formal title, it's easy to share it with someone when describing yourself. You likely studied for a field, joined an organization, and moved forward through recognizable stages while receiving promotions, titles, and responsibilities that signaled your progress along the way. Over time, the answer to that simple question began to explain far more than your daily activity; it suggested how you fit into the larger world.

The answer to that question is so telling, there are even experts in the field to help you design your response. Years ago, when I hosted a nationally syndicated radio show, I interviewed thousands of guests about leadership, entrepreneurship, psychology, and human behavior. One of those guests was Jim Beach, an entrepreneur who spent much of his career teaching people how to develop what many call an elevator pitch. The idea is simple. If you meet someone briefly, perhaps in an elevator or at a conference reception, you should be able to explain who you are and what you do in 15 seconds or so. Your goal is not to give a speech. Your goal is to say something memorable enough so that the other person asks you a follow-up question.

Jim described the elevator pitch as a kind of calling card. In a few sentences, you can communicate your credibility, establish value, and give someone a reason to keep the conversation going. In business settings people often call it a "value proposition," a phrase I hear so frequently that it can feel overused. The idea behind it is understandable, though. Because when an opportunity to connect with someone moves so quickly, you want to be able to explain who you are and why what you do matters. This is especially true if you are selling something.

Not long after having Jim on my show, someone asked me, "What do you do?" and I explained that I was a keynote speaker, had hosted a radio show for years, interviewed thousands of people, and spent much of my career studying behavioral research and curiosity in the workplace. At that moment, I realized that my answer was a mouthful and I probably needed to create a better elevator pitch.

It struck me how bad I was at summarizing my role, my accomplishments, and my professional identity. I found it challenging to compress what I "did" into a short description of what I do.

People spend an enormous amount of time refining those few sentences because the answer to that question carries so much meaning. The question communicates far more than we realize because it shares our identity.

"What do you do?" began to mean, "Who are you?"

Anyone who has worked on their elevator pitch likely pays attention to how people describe what they do. You might notice someone introduces themselves as a physician, an engineer, a teacher, or a consultant. Another person says they are an entrepreneur, a writer, or a manager. The title quickly becomes the most recognizable way to understand where someone fits in the world.

The question feels natural because for generations, modern life has been organized around our occupations. Schools prepared students for specific roles, organizations created ladders people were expected to climb, and titles became signals that told others how far someone had progressed. Those titles came to represent your expertise, credibility, and achievement in ways that were widely understood. When you handed someone a business card, the title printed on it communicated how others should interpret your contribution and where you likely fit within the larger system.

If you want a vivid example of how powerful those signals can become, think about the famous business card scene in the film *American Psycho*. People who have seen the movie almost always remember that moment. Christian Bale's character and his colleagues gather around a conference table comparing business cards with almost ceremonial intensity. They obsess over the color of the paper, the weight of the card, the font choice, and most of all, the title printed beneath their names. Each of them is a "Vice President" at the same firm, Pierce & Pierce, which reveals how interchangeable they are. Yet the men treat the cards as if they are measuring instruments of status. When one character produces a slightly thicker card with a subtle watermark, Bale's character nearly loses his composure trying to hide his envy. The moment is darkly funny, which is exactly why audiences remember it.

The scene works because it exaggerates something that exists in real life. Titles, credentials, and small symbols that signal achievement can become powerful markers of our identity. People compare them, measure progress through them, and sometimes defend them as if those markers say something essential about who they are. The humor in the scene comes from how seriously the characters treat something that small, yet it also reflects a pattern that has shaped how many people think about success, contribution, and recognition for decades.

If you can't relate to that scene, it may simply reflect that you have not spent much time in corporate environments. It is worth noting that the intended audience of this book is not just businesspeople. Many people reading this may be working in organizations, but others may not. Some may be students trying to imagine their future, and some may be raising families or caring for others. Some may be retired, volunteering, creating, learning, or simply searching for the next stage of life. The question of identity does not only belong to the working world. The deeper theme of this book is about how you find meaning through how you contribute, follow your curiosity, and develop your purpose both inside and outside of formal work.

Understanding that broader purpose helps explain why the roles people hold have carried such meaning. Within the system we created, for those in the working world, occupation gradually became far more than a way to earn income; it evolved into one of the main structures people used to explain adulthood and progress. Career milestones came to represent achievement. When you received a promotion, it signaled forward movement, and your eventual retirement marked the closing chapter of a long professional journey. Even dissatisfaction with work still fit inside that framework, because there was usually another stage ahead to pursue. Whether you worked in an office, ran a business, taught in a classroom, stayed home raising children, volunteered in a community, or studied in school preparing for the future, the role you held often became the easiest way to explain where you fit and how you contributed.

That is why the question, "What do you do?" feels more personal than it sounds.

When someone asks that question, most people immediately begin thinking about how their answer will be interpreted. The response can seem to carry signals about stability, progress, competence, and relevance, even when the conversation is casual. If you happen to be between roles, your sense of discomfort when sharing that can surface quickly, and if you are considering a transition or redefining what you want to do next, the uncertainty can feel surprisingly personal. In moments like that, a question that sounded harmless a minute earlier can suddenly feel less like small talk and more like a spotlight.

For much of the twentieth century, the link between your identity and your occupation felt reliable. You likely spent considerable time accumulating skills and experience. If you remained in a field for many years, it suggested that you were dedicated and competent. Even when industries evolved, they often changed slowly enough that most people could adapt without redefining themselves completely. You could update your expertise without reconsidering your entire identity.

Today, that stability feels less certain. After I present my keynotes or teach classes, people often approach me with questions that carry their deeper concerns. Many of them ask what I believe artificial intelligence will do to their profession. Some people wonder whether the work they spent decades mastering will still be valued in the future. If they are younger professionals, they might ask whether the career path they just started will exist 20 years from now.

Lately, their questions usually revolve around intelligent systems. Their underlying concern is not just about the technology. It is about what will happen to their identity due to that technology.

If the work you trained for begins to change, where does that leave you? If intelligent systems perform tasks that once required years of training, what happens to the value of all the experience you built along the way? If the structure that once organized your days evolves or disappears, how do you understand your place without it?

I have heard versions of those concerns from people at every stage of life. Senior executives sometimes wonder how their influence will evolve as systems become more automated. Mid-career professionals occasionally question whether their expertise will even be needed in their field. Even people who have already retired often admit that when the emails stop and the calendar looks empty, they discover how much identity had been wrapped around the title they once carried.

In some ways, the conversation reminds me of what people experienced in the 1980s when computers first began appearing in offices. At that time, I was selling computer software to school districts, and I often met people who had never worked with a computer before. For many of them, the technology felt unfamiliar and unsettling. Some worried openly that automation would eliminate large numbers of administrative roles or replace work that had always been done by people. It was hard to blame them, because they saw people who had been part of typing pools lose their jobs, they saw accounting systems become automated, and entire departments reorganized as digital tools slowly replaced manual processes.

Those changes felt dramatic to the people experiencing them. Yet history shows that new roles emerged alongside the old ones. No one predicted titles like social media manager, data scientist, or user experience designer because the technologies that created those roles had not yet appeared. The systems adapted and new opportunities developed in ways few people anticipated.

What makes the current moment feel different is not simply the pace of technological progress but the scale of the changes we will experience. Today, respected leaders openly discuss the possibility that intelligent systems may perform analytical, creative, and strategic tasks that once seemed uniquely human.

When entrepreneurs like Elon Musk talk about artificial intelligence transforming industries, and warn that AI can replace nearly all jobs, the question turns to the future of human contribution.

Even if the most dramatic predictions never materialize, people will still worry about their stability. The uncertainty can be frightening. If you are a professional who spent decades building expertise, you may suddenly wonder whether that knowledge will remain valuable. Maybe you are a manager who built a career around decision-making and now notice that software can analyze information faster than you or your entire teams once could. Even creative professionals may watch algorithms generate ideas in seconds.

The issue is not just whether jobs disappear, because many or even most might. The bigger question is how you will handle those shifts. When your identity becomes tightly tied to your occupation, that kind of disruption can feel deeply personal because it threatens more than your income. It affects how you see yourself.

Having to learn something new can feel uncomfortable when it seems to suggest that the previous version of you is no longer enough. That reaction often has more to do with protecting your identity than resisting change. Part of the reason this reaction is so strong is that the pattern has been reinforced for years. Early on in schools, many people are encouraged to choose a direction and stay with it, select a major, build a résumé, and move step by step along a recognizable path of advancement. Titles, responsibilities, and recognition become the signals that confirm your progress, and as those markers accumulate, the role you hold gradually becomes the easiest way others measure your achievement.

Yet your identity has always been broader than the work you do.

Long before formal careers organized modern life, people experienced meaning through family, community, creativity, learning, and shared responsibility. Industrial economies compressed many of those dimensions into professional labels because labels were easier to measure and reward. The question now is whether that compression continues to serve us in a world where roles evolve more quickly and an individual's contribution may appear in many different forms.

If intelligent systems continue changing how tasks are performed, what you do for a living may become a less stable anchor for how you interpret your identity. In that future, you likely will contribute across multiple domains at once. You might teach, mentor, design, volunteer, invest, write, or build something new without fitting neatly inside a single job description. In that context, answering the question, "What do you do?" with one thing will begin to feel incomplete.

One way to handle this change is to broaden what your identity is built on. Instead of anchoring your entire identity to a title, you can begin noticing patterns of how your adaptive curiosity impacts what you contribute, and your capabilities that impact different parts of your life. To adapt to this change, you will need to ask yourself some revealing questions: What kinds of problems consistently draw your attention? What activities energize you enough that you return to them again and again? Where do other people seem to benefit from what you naturally enjoy doing?

When your identity rests on a wider selection of activities and someone asks you that familiar question, "What do you do?" it now will become more of an opening for a conversation rather than a verdict of how valuable you are. In that reality, you can describe your current role without it defining the entirety of who you are. You can acknowledge transitions without feeling diminished and explore new directions without thinking that reinvention erases your past.

This is where the idea of adaptive curiosity begins to emerge.

In my earlier book, *Cracking the Curiosity Code*, I explored curiosity as a driver of learning, innovation, and engagement. In this book, I introduced my research regarding the factors that inhibit curiosity, including how to overcome them to get out of status-quo thinking. Later, I wrote *Curiosity Unleashed* to address the questions I received after keynotes or corporate training events. Many of those questions revolved around how to develop a culture of curiosity and measure the financial impact of doing so. Additionally, that book shared examples of people and organizations that either succeeded or failed based on whether they embraced curiosity.

In *Adaptive Curiosity*, my goal is to expand the concept of curiosity even further. When you develop adaptive curiosity, you become willing to examine who you are beyond a title and explore what gives you meaning rather than waiting for institutions to tell you what direction you should take. Adaptive curiosity invites you to notice where your interests, abilities, and opportunities intersect so that you can design meaningful contribution even when familiar structures evolve.

The next chapters explore how your identity became so closely tied to your occupation and why that connection feels so strong today. You will examine how to experiment with new forms of contribution, reconnect with sources of meaning that extend beyond your title, and design a life that remains purposeful even as the structure of your work changes.

For now, begin with a simple observation. The next time someone asks what you do, notice your reaction. Do you answer quickly? Do you pause to consider how your response will sound? Do you feel pride, uncertainty, or a brief moment of hesitation?

That small moment reveals something important. It shows how closely your identity and occupation have become linked in the way many of us think about ourselves.

For generations, that connection shaped how people explained their place in the world. The question now is whether the answer will always be limited to a title, or if people will start describing themselves in broader ways that reflect curiosity, contribution, and purpose across different parts of life.

To understand why this shift feels so unsettling today, it helps to look at the stability people once expected.

CHAPTER 2

The Stability People Expected

When I was growing up, people talked about stability with admiration. If someone stayed at the same company for 20 or 30 years, it meant they had done well in life. It suggested they were responsible, successful, and had a clear sense of direction. Most people believed that if you worked hard, chose a sensible path, and stayed committed, your life would unfold in a fairly predictable way.

At that time, there was a strong expectation that once you obtained a secure job, you stayed. Working somewhere for less than a few years could raise eyebrows. No one wanted to be seen as a job-hopper, and leaving a stable role often felt risky even if you believed it was the right decision.

That same desire for stability exists outside of work, too. A student who changes majors may feel their choice to pursue a new path somehow let someone down. An employee retraining for a new certification may feel that it will open a door to something unknown, which can make them uneasy. Even a parent returning to the workforce after years at home may feel uncomfortable. The circumstances differ, but the underlying uncertainty feels remarkably similar.

Our education system reinforced the same pattern. The goal for many of us was to earn a degree that led to a profession, and if you went to graduate school, that expanded your opportunities for leadership or specialization. Many people went on to earn certifications to validate their expertise. When someone invested years in training, the assumption was that they would practice that skill for a long time.

Under those conditions, specializing deeply made sense. You could devote your energy to mastering a narrow area because the field itself seemed unlikely to disappear. Industries changed slowly enough that people could adapt without reinventing themselves entirely.

That expectation of stability also shaped how people interpreted risk. Leaving a secure role meant giving up very real benefits. I felt the anxiety that many others experienced when doing so. When I left a major pharmaceutical company after working there for nearly 20 years, I walked away from five weeks of vacation, a company car, excellent benefits, and a generous retirement match. I had earned several President's Circle sales trips where I traveled to places like Hawaii and St. Thomas. Sales meetings took us to cities like New Orleans and Orlando, and people like Bob Newhart and Jay Leno entertained our group. From the outside, it looked like an ideal situation.

Many people told me directly that I was crazy to leave. Others did not say it out loud, but their reactions when I explained what I was doing made this obvious. Losing the company car seemed to be the detail that convinced most people that I had made a mistake. More than one person told me they would gladly trade jobs with me. To many people, that position represented the definition of stability.

What they could not see was what it felt like to do work that did not align with my passions or sense of meaning. Stability was there, but fulfillment was not, at least not for me. I always preferred a more administrative role. The thought of driving around all day, especially in the summer in the Phoenix area, was not my idea of how I wanted to spend my time. Getting in and out of a hot car all day can be tough when it gets close to 120 degrees outside. Having come from a job selling software,

I knew I wanted to work in an office setting. But, leaving that job meant starting over in a commission-based position in a small two-person loan office. Going from a six-figure salary to the potential of making nothing at all was unsettling, to say the least, since I had children, a house, and responsibilities.

What I hadn't considered was how much it impacted how people saw me when they asked that all-important question, "What do you do?" I went from saying I worked for a major pharmaceutical manufacturer to explaining that I was a loan officer in a tiny office. The contrast made the decision feel even riskier. I felt like I had to explain my decision, even though I made it willingly, especially when I saw the look on people's faces who knew what I had previously done for employment.

I understood why others found it hard to grasp why I would leave. If you grew up in that environment, stability could start to feel almost magnetic. Once you were inside a system that seemed reliable, it made sense to stay there. Part of that pull came from loyalty, but part of it came from something more personal. When the next step is obvious to achieve, your life can feel easier to organize, because you know what you are working toward. When you receive promotions, achieve milestones, and eventually head into retirement, that direction helps you feel that life is unfolding the way it is supposed to.

You probably heard the same advice many people did: Do not reinvent the wheel. If someone already figured out the right path, the sensible thing was to follow it. That thinking, at least in terms of career paths, can work well for many people when systems remain stable for long periods of time. Yet you may have noticed another side to it. Solving something yourself has its own kind of satisfaction. Watching someone else solve a Rubik's Cube might be impressive, but the real thrill comes when you finally solve it on your own.

I felt that thrill after leaving pharmaceutical sales. I had spent years becoming the person who knew almost everything about my role. Suddenly, I was the opposite. I had stepped into a completely different field and knew almost nothing. At first, that realization was intimidating. There is a moment when you leave something familiar and think, "What in the world was I thinking?" and realize you are starting from the beginning again. Yet for me, the feeling quickly turned from frightening to energizing. Discovering something new became addictive. It might have seemed like I was facing a steep climb to get somewhere, but rather than allowing someone else to place me on a mountain, I climbed it and the experience of reaching the summit made the effort feel worthwhile.

Once I absorbed everything I could about a new challenge and began to master it, I felt ready for the next one. I started changing directions more often, almost like a sponge soaking up knowledge in one area before moving on to the next. At one point I even decided to pursue a Ph.D., partly because I wanted to see how difficult it would be. It turns out that challenge was very real. Still, the process reinforced something important: Discovery can be more motivating than stability.

That realization helped me see something more clearly. For a long time, people have felt a tension between two instincts. One is the pull toward exploration, discovery, and trying something new. The other is the pull toward stability and the sense of security that comes from staying with something familiar.

If you grew up hearing stories about how adulthood was supposed to unfold, stability was usually at the center of that picture. Your loyalty was rewarded. Retirement often followed decades of service and pensions are still one of the clearest signals that the system was built around continuity.

The message has always been simple: Invest in the institution and the institution would invest in you.

I am one of the few people I know who receives a pension, and I appreciate it. At the same time, I sometimes wonder what opportunities might have appeared if I had left my pharmaceutical job earlier. Stability offers benefits, but it also creates tradeoffs.

When you hear the same message from families, schools, and workplaces, it starts to feel like that is just how life works.

Few of us have ever stopped to question whether the structure itself might eventually change. For a long time, it did not seem necessary to ask that question.

But that sense of stability always depended on certain conditions to remain. It relied on economic systems, technologies, and institutions that supported long-term continuity. As long as those conditions remained steady, the expectation held. Now, those conditions are changing.

The pace of change right now has accelerated dramatically. Digital tools have transformed nearly every industry. Intelligent systems now perform tasks that once required people to have specialized expertise, causing entire industries to be redesigned.

If you grew up believing that stability would naturally follow your commitment and hard work, this shift can feel unsettling. The path that once seemed obvious to you can now appear less defined, and skills that took years to develop can sometimes be supplemented, or even replaced, by software in seconds.

That concern many of you feel as you watch this unfold is about your identity.

You may start to notice this shift in everyday life. Some people are organizing their lives around projects, causes, learning, or creative pursuits. You might find yourself moving between different responsibilities and roles instead of one role that felt permanent. Many of you will build a series of experiences that connect in unexpected ways.

If you expected stability to come from staying in one place, this shift can feel uncomfortable. For others, it has already become normal.

You can feel the psychological impact of that change quickly. For a moment, assume intelligent machines do most of the work humans have done. It's possible that by the time you read this, that has happened. But consider this: When you build plans around continuity, rapid change introduces ambiguity. Instead of asking which rung on the ladder comes next, you may now be asking which problems deserve your attention. Instead of focusing only on advancement inside one institution, you can consider how your abilities can translate across different contexts.

This shift pushes you to think about stability differently, and it is where adaptive curiosity begins to matter. In earlier decades, stability meant remaining inside a durable structure. Today, stability increasingly comes from your ability to be adaptable and rely on yourself rather than an organization to determine your future. Your sense of security will begin to grow from your ability to learn, adjust, and remain engaged as the world adjusts to a new reality where intelligent machines do more than we did in the past.

When your sense of stability begins to depend on your adaptability, learning naturally becomes more of a continuous process. How you view your growth might shift from thinking about potential promotions to thinking what you can contribute that is meaningful. That contribution may shift across multiple projects, communities, and roles rather than inside a single hierarchy.

Your life can begin to look less like a straight line and more like an evolving path.

You may already recognize parts of this transition in your own life. I know I have. When I interview leaders, those conversations often become material I share with students, ideas I write about, and insights I use in keynote presentations. In my interviews, I never intentionally tried to get leaders to share their ideas, but now I see how so many unrelated things I do reinforce one another.

When you realize you can combine your interests, abilities, and experiences in different ways, you begin to see value in doing more than one thing rather than staying confined to a single lane.

At first, that freedom can feel disorienting. Without a clearly defined ladder, you must decide what progress looks like for you. That responsibility requires you to use intentional thinking and ask yourself some helpful questions.

Which challenges in your work, home, classroom, or community matter to you?

Which abilities do you have that are worth developing further?

Where does your effort create the most meaningful impact?

Answering those questions requires examining any assumptions you have about success that may have formed under very different conditions.

Stability provides clarity and comfort for many people, and the desire for it has not disappeared. It is simply evolving and requires more input from you than from outside organizations or structures.

Stability can still exist in a changing world, but it depends more on how you respond than on how fixed the surrounding structures remain. This requires you to embrace adaptive curiosity, the ability to stay open, keep learning, and keep contributing even when familiar structures change. Tools and systems will continue evolving without your input, but how you will interact with them remains your choice.

There is opportunity inside that transition. When paths are less rigid, this allows your creativity to flourish. You can design combinations of roles that reflect your strengths, pursue projects that align with your emerging interests, and build relationships across disciplines and communities.

Instead of waiting for a predefined opening, you can begin creating openings for yourself.

Uncertainty then begins to serve a different role as it becomes a signal that exploration is required. When you explore, it strengthens your capability, which builds confidence and allows you to contribute in a changing world.

I remember how unsettling starting over felt. Yet that discomfort eventually turned into excitement as I learned new skills and explored unfamiliar territory. The path that followed led to far more interesting and meaningful work than I could have imagined at the time.

If you are leaving a predictable structure, it can change how you see your own competence. Your stability will grow from your ability to keep learning, to connect ideas across different experiences, and to remain engaged.

Even if you have been told to find something reliable, stay committed, and build your life around a familiar structure, you might also recognize moments in your own life when learning something new, changing direction, or exploring an unfamiliar challenge brought a different kind of energy. Those moments often show you just how powerful discovery can be when it becomes part of your daily life.

As you reflect on your own expectations about stability and your future, it may be useful to ask which assumptions still serve you and which ones might need reconsideration. When you do that, you begin building a foundation capable of supporting whatever paths unfold next.

CHAPTER 3

When Expertise Feels Uncertain

Take a moment and think about something you do well. It's a good feeling, isn't it? Most people develop a strong sense of confidence around the things they have practiced or worked on for years. In the workplace, you might be someone who people go to because you can step in without hesitation when others are unsure. With enough experience, your competence becomes second nature. You might notice that you begin to anticipate problems before they surface and recognize patterns quickly. When you reach that level of expertise, it creates a sense of internal stability and allows you to walk into a room without wondering whether you belong there.

When you have invested years in becoming good at something, you expect those abilities to remain relevant. You sacrificed other opportunities, practiced until difficult things became instinctive, and built confidence through repetition. When a tool suddenly does part of that skill in a single command, it feels personal. The disruption often triggers an emotional response because competence has always been closely tied to how people see themselves.

Periods of transition can shake that confidence. When you move into a new role or when your work changes unexpectedly, you may suddenly find yourself rebuilding the sense of certainty you once carried easily. I discovered this firsthand when I left my position as an MBA Program Chair at a local university.

I loved teaching, and one of my favorite parts of the role involved interviewing remarkable people who came to speak at the university. Those conversations energized me. I enjoyed learning from leaders across many industries, and I knew that if I left academia, I would miss that experience.

Eventually, I decided to focus more seriously on becoming a motivational keynote speaker. While preparing my website, my developer suggested adding more audio and video content. I agreed to be interviewed about my work, assuming it would simply provide useful material for the site. During that conversation, I learned that the person interviewing me hosted a nationally syndicated talk show. Having just experienced interviewing some interesting people in my previous role, I was curious about his job, so I asked how he landed that position, and he told me the radio station was looking for additional hosts.

That sounded like a fascinating opportunity, so I decided, in addition to my speaking and writing, that it would be a natural fit to host a show as well. There was only one problem. I had two weeks to learn how to put it all together.

This was before platforms like Zoom made recording effortless. I had no idea how to route calls through a phone line and capture them on a computer. I did not understand audio levels or how to manage timing, transitions, or the deal with the unpredictability of live interviews. In a matter of days, I went from feeling competent in a structured academic environment to feeling like a complete beginner in a technical and public one.

I didn't have a lot of time to worry about whether I made the right decision, but I knew I needed to sink or swim. My experience up until this point was not exactly helpful when it came to learning how to do all those technical things and I faced a steep learning curve.

Those early weeks tested my ego and forced me to confront something many people experience when their expertise is shaken. I forgot to hit record on occasion. One guest, who unfortunately was a time management expert, was understandably less than thrilled when I asked if he would allow me to interview him again because I had forgotten to capture the first conversation. I struggled with sound quality, scheduling, and the mechanics of inserting advertising into the program. I could have interpreted those moments as evidence that I did not belong in that space. Instead, I chose to treat them as part of building a new kind of expertise.

The most difficult part was getting over myself. When you are used to being good at something, making mistakes can feel uncomfortable. Yet when you are producing several shows each week, perfection simply is not possible.

My good friend and Hall of Fame speaker Ford Saeks often says, "Done is better than perfect." Accepting that idea was challenging. For competitive people, perfection often feels like proof that we deserve to be there. Yet waiting until everything felt perfect would have prevented me from ever stepping behind that microphone. For many of us, progress requires accepting imperfection long enough to improve.

That period of rapid learning was uncomfortable, but it was also rewarding. Each small technical success built my confidence. Each interview strengthened my ability to listen carefully and guide a conversation in real time. I was no longer relying on credentials or titles to prove my expertise. Instead, I was developing it again through experience.

Looking back, that experience made it clear to me that our expertise does not stay frozen in time. It changes as the world around us changes.

You can see how expertise can be impacted by intelligent machines across many professions today. Teachers who might have spent decades refining lessons can now utilize software to put together lesson plans in seconds. Truck drivers who once relied solely on instinct now navigate digital logistics systems that optimize routes automatically. Even parents returning to the workforce after years at home often discover that entire workflows have moved online.

In each case, the experience people built over time still matters. What changes is how that experience now gets used.

Moments like these often force you to reconsider your identity. You may still be experienced in many ways, yet at the same time you find yourself learning again. Being experienced and a beginner at the same time takes humility and curiosity.

When your confidence has been anchored to a specific skill, changes in the environment can make that anchor feel unstable. Some people respond by retreating into what they already know and criticizing new technologies. Others rush to master every emerging tool. Both reactions are understandable, because in both cases what is really being challenged is your identity.

When your expertise becomes uncertain, reinvention can feel personal because competence represents years of effort and proof of ability. If technology accelerates part of that competence, you may question where your value now resides. The answer rarely lies in competing with the tool. It lies in expanding your role around it.

You might have been told that the ones who will eventually have any of the jobs that are left will be the creative people. That might be partially true, but I have heard entertainers worry that artificial intelligence will eventually create digital versions of them as well. We already have seen that technology can replicate some of their creativity, but it cannot replicate lived experience or the human perspective behind creative work.

When researchers analyzed the late comedian George Carlin's comedy and generated material in his style, they reproduced elements of his voice and rhythm remarkably well. Yet something was missing. It sounded a lot like him and even had a lot of his way of arranging a joke, but it was still off. It was hard to really put a finger on what was different, but it was clear it was not George. That difference reminds us that machines can imitate patterns, but they cannot replace the human perspective that gives those patterns meaning.

Consider writing as another example. If you do any writing as part of your day, you know that a generative AI system can assemble sentences quickly, but it cannot draw from your personal experience or understanding of a particular audience who will read your work as well as you can. AI can produce words, but the human perspective can provide much more to shape the meaning and connection to those words.

You see the same pattern across fields like law, medicine, engineering, finance, and education. Intelligent systems handle repetition efficiently, but interpretation still requires human judgment. When a system analyzes information, the expert decides what it means and what should happen next.

If you are used to being an expert in your field, adjusting to that kind of change takes humility. It means acknowledging that part of your previous skill set may no longer be the primary differentiator. This requires you to let yourself learn again and occasionally sit in rooms where someone else understands the new system better than you do.

If your confidence is built on certainty, that can fall apart quickly. When you build confidence based on adaptability, it tends to last longer because it comes from knowing you can keep learning.

When I stepped into radio with only two weeks of preparation, I did not lose the abilities I had developed earlier in academia and speaking. I brought curiosity and the ability to communicate well with another person. Those qualities helped me build the technical skills I needed that led to a long-running successful show.

The skills you have developed will follow you on your path into whatever you choose to do next. The thinking skills, emotional intelligence, and resilience you have cultivated do not disappear simply because a tool can perform part of the work faster. If you define yourself only by a narrow capability, you will find that change feels threatening. If you define yourself by your ability to learn and adapt, your new skills and abilities will help you remain relevant.

If you are feeling unsettled now, thinking your expertise is not as in demand as it once was, it does not mean you are finished. In many cases, it is the beginning of discovering new ways you can contribute.

As adults, we sometimes underestimate how much our identity becomes wrapped inside our competence. When you are young, experimentation is expected of you. You are supposed to try different activities, make mistakes, and gradually learn what you enjoy. As your experience accumulates, expectations of you change and others begin to rely on your consistency. Because of that, beginning again later in life can feel far more uncomfortable than it did when you were 20.

Part of the discomfort comes from how we compare ourselves. When you measure your early attempts in a new area against skills developed over decades in another, the gap can feel enormous. What we often forget is that our earlier ability to master something also began awkwardly. It improved through repetition, feedback, and time.

Once you recognize that progress involves participating in this pattern, reinvention becomes easier to accept. The discipline, work ethic, and pattern recognition you developed earlier do not disappear; they carry over into what you learn next. They may not remove the beginner stage, but they often shorten it. That is why people who stay open to learning throughout their careers tend to evolve rather than remain stagnated.

This is where adaptability begins to matter more than certainty. When expertise becomes uncertain, you face a choice. You can protect what you have already built and hope the environment stabilizes around it, or you can expand your range and explore new ways to contribute. Adaptive curiosity favors the second path because it treats change as an invitation to grow rather than encouraging you to give up.

As you examine your own expertise, consider where you may be holding onto a definition that once served you but now feels limiting. Notice when learning something new feels intimidating yet energizing. Pay attention to moments when your need for perfectionism might be holding you back from participating.

When your expertise keeps evolving, people continue to trust it because it shows growth rather than clinging to the past.

Something else tends to happen as your expertise shifts. Work that once took up most of the day may now take far less time. At first, this new efficiency can feel like relief, but after a while it can also begin to feel like something is missing.

When the work you were known for no longer fills your day the way it once did, the structure of your schedule starts to change. The calendar that used to stay packed begins to open, and you may notice gaps where work used to be.

Open space sounds appealing at first, yet it becomes more complicated when you realize that you are the one responsible for figuring out what to do with it.

Losing certainty about your expertise is one challenge, but facing unstructured time is another. When no one assigns the next task and your progress is no longer measured by a visible output alone, you recognize something: What you know is only as important as how you choose to use it to find meaning in your time.

When that moment of recognition arrives, the most helpful response is not to panic or give up, but to rely on your adaptive curiosity. Instead of assuming that change has taken something away from you, curiosity invites you to ask new questions. What abilities do you still carry that matter in this environment? Where might those abilities be applied in new ways? What could you learn next that would expand what you can do?

Adaptive curiosity provides the willingness to stay open, keep learning, and continue exploring possibilities even when the structures around you begin to shift. It allows you to recognize the uncertainty and treat it as useful information. It also helps you see how you can grow within changing conditions rather than waiting for the conditions to stabilize.

Throughout history, the people who adapted most successfully were rarely those who resisted change the longest. They were the ones who remained curious enough to examine what was happening and flexible enough to adjust their thinking.

Adaptive curiosity allows you to experiment, gather evidence, and gradually rebuild confidence in unfamiliar territory.

Understanding why adaptive curiosity becomes so powerful in moments like this requires looking more closely at how it works. When your expertise no longer feels as useful as it once did, your curiosity can guide you toward new forms of contribution, learning, and meaning. Many people gradually lose touch with the level of curiosity they had when they were young and settle into routines, yet the ability to ask better questions and explore new possibilities never disappears. When people learn how to strengthen that curiosity again, they often move through periods of change with far more confidence than they expected.

CHAPTER 4

The Problem of Too Much Free Time

If you have ever worked in a job that you didn't love, you probably counted the days until Friday. You aren't alone when you consider how many people say, thank God it's Friday or TGIF. The phrase became so common that a restaurant even built an entire brand around it. For many people, Friday represents relief because the workweek is finally over and two days of freedom are ahead with no alarm clock, no commute, and no deadlines demanding their attention.

It's not just Fridays that can create a sense of what to expect. Earlier in my career, Sunday nights used to bring a completely different feeling than they do for me now. Instead of relaxing and enjoying my day off, I often felt that familiar dread about Monday morning. If you have ever experienced that feeling, you know exactly what I mean. Now that I genuinely love what I do, it's so different. I look forward to Mondays because the start of the week means new conversations, new problems to solve, and new ideas to explore. That contrast raises an interesting question. What if more days felt like that second experience instead of the first? What if life becomes less about waiting for Friday and more about being curious about what tomorrow might bring?

That question matters more now because technology and efficiency are changing the way people spend their time. If intelligent systems begin handling more of the tasks you once had to do yourself, you might suddenly have far more open hours than you are used to having. At first that can sound wonderful, but the reality becomes more complicated when you stop and think about what open time feels like when it is not filled with a sense of challenge, direction, or connection.

I wish I could say all my jobs felt rewarding, and that time flew by without me realizing it. This wasn't my experience early in my career when I worked as a temporary employee. In the 1980s they called us Kelly Girls. Later the company removed the gendered language, but that was the term at the time. I would move from office to office filling in for people who were out sick or on vacation. The work itself was rarely challenging. What I remember most clearly was waiting for five o'clock so I could finally go home.

Most days, I sat at a desk with almost nothing to do, essentially serving as a warm body in a chair waiting for the phone to ring or for someone to walk over with a small task like typing a short memo. Because there was no real direction, no challenge, and no sense that I was building anything meaningful, I spent a great deal of time watching the clock and counting down the minutes until the workday ended. It was brutal because time seemed to move so slowly and I just wanted someone to give me more to do.

Fortunately, most of my jobs after that one kept me busier. After several decades of working full time, I decided to take some time off. My kids were grown and I thought it might be fun to enroll in cooking classes. Immediately, I felt uncomfortable and told myself I was simply bored, yet after a while I realized something else was going on. What I was really feeling was loneliness combined with a lack of direction. When no one is asking for your input or effort, and no meaningful challenge excites you, the hours stretch out in ways that brought me back to feeling like I did in my Kelly Girls days.

This is the problem with having too much free time. The discomfort comes from finding yourself alone with that time and no clear sense of what to do with it.

For most of modern history, people rarely faced this problem because their schedules were already full. You had work schedules, school calendars, commutes, deadlines, and expectations that carried you through your day. You woke up knowing what was required and where you needed to be, and that structure moved you from one commitment to the next. Even when work felt repetitive, the rhythm of activity created momentum, and at the end of the day you could look back and see what you had completed, which made it easier to believe you had made progress.

When that structure changes, however, something interesting begins to happen. You start turning inward and questions that once stayed in the background of your mind begin to surface. You may start wondering what you are actually building toward, what kinds of activities energize you, and what makes a day feel meaningful.

I experienced that when I took that time off. After many years working in lending and real estate, the idea of taking a break sounded wonderful. The cooking classes weren't as I imagined. I pictured relaxed afternoons learning new recipes while enjoying the freedom of having nowhere urgent to be. At first it felt like it was going to be a nice change of pace. It gave me time to create interesting meals for dinner that my husband loved, and I no longer had to deal with urgent emails, constant meetings, or the pressure of meeting sales quotas. For a little while, that extra time felt nice.

The problem for me was that my children were grown and my husband left for work each morning, which meant I spent much of the day by myself. I did not have a built-in reason to leave the house beyond the occasional class. In cooking school, many of the other students arrived in pairs or came with friends. When class ended, they walked out together talking about what they planned to cook for dinner, while I walked to the parking lot alone and drove home.

Free time feels very different when no one else is around to share it. If you are single, you might appreciate that time alone, but for me, I felt lonely and had no sense of direction or meaning. I started to notice that the only people I spoke with during the day were people I had to pay to be around me, such as the cooking instructor, my hairdresser, or the people who did my nails. Don't get me wrong, I had plenty of friends I could call, yet I have never particularly enjoyed long social lunches or spending a day chatting with friends, so I often found myself spending much of the day at home by myself.

Eventually, I realized I missed having a challenge, meaningful conversations, and the sense that I was working toward something alongside other people. Work had provided far more than income. It gave me intellectual stimulation, daily interaction with people I did not have to pay to spend time with me, and shared goals that required effort and collaboration. When those elements disappeared, the extra time did not create fulfillment for me. It showed me what I was missing.

Activity was not enough to make me feel inspired. I was missing the combination of challenge, connection, and contribution that had once shaped my days. When those ingredients disappear, time can begin to drag, and that reminds you how deeply purpose and interaction influence the way you feel about yourself and your life.

You might recognize that same experience during other transitions in your life. I was reminded of it recently when I was speaking at an event in Dubai and had the opportunity to go on stage right after tennis champion Andre Agassi. In his autobiography, Agassi openly admitted that he often did not love the sport that made him famous. Tennis gave him structure, recognition, and extraordinary success, yet it did not always provide the fulfillment people assumed it would. Hearing him talk about that experience reinforced something important. Even people who achieve remarkable success can eventually find themselves asking the same questions about meaning and direction the rest of us do.

You can see similar moments in many different stages of life. When a student leaves a tightly scheduled semester and suddenly faces an unstructured summer, the freedom can feel strange. When someone begins working remotely, the flexibility may feel exciting at first, yet over time they may notice how much daily interaction has disappeared. When children leave home, many parents look around the house and wonder what they are supposed to do with the space and time that has suddenly opened up.

In situations like these, people often describe the feeling as boredom, although boredom usually signals something deeper. It can reflect loneliness, the loss of momentum, or the absence of shared effort. Much of the connection people experience with others stems from routine activity. Offices create hallway conversations. Classrooms create shared experiences. And workplaces bring people together around common challenges. When those environments change, the small interactions that once happened naturally begin to fade, and the absence of those interactions can gradually affect how connected you feel to the world around you.

When long stretches of open time appear, your mind also has more room to wander. When I was growing up, adults often repeated the phrase that an idle mind is the devil's workshop. That was their way of telling you that if you are not engaged in something meaningful, your attention can drift toward things that are unproductive or worse. When you get all "up in your head," you start focusing on any concerns you have about your health, finances, relationships, or past decisions, and that can be unsettling. An unstructured day does not create those thoughts, but it gives them more room to grow.

Relationships can shift as well when schedules change. Couples who once spent most days apart may suddenly find themselves sharing far more time together. In some cases, that strengthens their connection, while in other cases it exposes differences that busy routines once made easier to overlook. Time tends to magnify whatever issues might already exist.

Another subtle change involves the signals that once told you your effort mattered. Completing tasks created a sense of competence, being needed reinforced relevance, and meeting deadlines confirmed that someone depended on your contribution. When those signals become less frequent, the sense of contribution begins to shift inward, and instead of asking what needs to be done next you may start asking a different question. What can I do that actually matters enough for me to give it my time?

When this happens, some people try to recreate the intensity they once experienced by adding projects, volunteer commitments, or new responsibilities that restore a sense of structure. Others drift into passive habits, spending hours moving through news, videos, or digital content that fills time without creating much satisfaction. Time passes either way, yet the experience of that time feels dramatically different.

What has really changed in these moments is responsibility. When your day is no longer organized by external demands, you become the person responsible for determining how that time is used. That shift can feel unfamiliar because most adults were trained to respond to structure created for them rather than creating it on their own.

When your schedule opens up and the usual demands stop filling every hour, you begin noticing thoughts and feelings that were easy to ignore when your life was busier. Dissatisfaction, anxiety, or ambition may become more visible. Instead of viewing those reactions as problems to eliminate, it can be more useful to treat them as signals about what your life may be missing. Loneliness may point to the need for stronger community, restlessness often points to the absence of challenge, and dissatisfaction can signal there is still something in you that wants to learn, explore, or grow. Your curiosity may be sitting there waiting, but you may not know where to focus it.

As technology and efficiency impact your daily life, you may eventually discover how much work occupies less of your time than it once did. That possibility raises an important question: What will you do with the hours that open up in your schedule? Some of you will drift through that time without much direction, while others of you will begin searching for challenges that make you feel alive again.

I can tell you from experience that meaningful work does not always require a paycheck. When I began focusing on my writing and speaking about curiosity, I spent enormous stretches of time working at my computer. There were days when I would sit there for 12 hours or more without realizing how much time had passed. No one assigned that work, and for a long time, no one paid me for it. I simply felt driven to explore the ideas.

That was a far cry from my time watching the clock slowly tick by earlier in my career. When something genuinely captures your curiosity, time behaves differently. Hours pass quickly because you are absorbed in what you are doing, and instead of wondering when the day will end, you often wish you had more time to keep going.

The real challenge for you and many others in the future may not be the lack of work. You might like that at first. The challenge will be learning how to fill your time with activities that engage your mind, stretch your abilities, and give your effort a sense of direction. If work stops organizing most of your day, the question becomes what you will choose to organize it around and whether you will design a life that feels meaningful rather than waiting for something to fill the hours.

CHAPTER 5

When Distraction Replaces Satisfaction

I have always loved technology, probably because I grew up watching shows that imagined the future long before it arrived. One of my favorite shows was *The Wild Wild West*, which was technically about the old West but managed to incorporate high technology devices that felt completely out of place in that setting. Seeing futuristic inventions in the middle of the old West was very cutting edge at that time.

I also loved *The Jetsons*, which was a cartoon version of a 1950s family living in the future. They had flying cars, robots who helped around the house, and gadgets that handled ordinary chores. George Jetson was a bit of a lovable oaf, the kind of character you could imagine in a modern animated show like *Family Guy*, yet technology surrounded everything his family did.

My favorite show had to be *Star Trek*. The creator, Gene Roddenberry, seemed to predict technology decades before any of it was invented. When you look back at the original series from the 1960s, it is remarkable how many ideas he imagined that are now a reality. In the show, they had devices that looked like early versions of flip phones, voice-controlled computers, tablets, and video communication. I loved the creativity of those ideas. I am still waiting for someone to create a transporter device so that we can transport ourselves to another destination thousands of miles away in just a few seconds.

What all those shows had in common was a hopeful view of the impact of technology on the future. The machines were impressive, but they never replaced what made the characters human. In *The Wild Wild West*, Jim West and Artemus Gordon used their inventions to outsmart the bad guys. In *The Jetsons*, George Jetson relied on gadgets to make his everyday life easier. And in *Star Trek*, the crew of the Enterprise used technology to explore, discover, and solve problems. In every case, the tools supported human effort rather than replacing it.

What I never imagined was a future where technology would become so good at capturing attention that it could end up filling entire days without asking anything meaningful from us in return.

Today, you can pick up a phone and begin scrolling through an endless stream of information, entertainment, and commentary. One video leads to another. A headline pulls you into a comment thread. A photo becomes a short clip, which leads to another suggestion chosen by an algorithm that already knows how to keep you watching. You may sit wanting to look at something for five minutes and suddenly notice that an hour has disappeared.

Most people have had that experience. You glance at the clock and wonder where the time went. Your mind stayed engaged the entire time because something new kept appearing on the screen. Yet when you finally put the device down, you might have asked yourself: What did that hour actually give me?

This is not about criticizing technology itself. Digital tools can expand creativity, accelerate learning, and connect people across the world in ways that would have seemed impossible only a few decades ago. The issue is how easily distraction becomes the default when nothing else is directing your attention.

If technology gives you more open hours in your day, you become responsible for deciding where your attention goes. In that open space, distraction often becomes the easiest option because it requires almost no effort to begin. You simply pick up a device and start scrolling, and before long, the minutes begin stacking into hours.

At first, that might feel harmless or even relaxing. You might tell yourself that you deserve a break after years of working hard. I recently had someone say to me that if intelligent machines replace all jobs, he would be thrilled spending his days gaming, watching shows, and scrolling through social media. From where he stands today, that kind of life might sound appealing. He worked very hard and is likely in need of some kind of break. Anyone who has ever felt exhausted from work can understand why the idea of unlimited free time sounds attractive.

The real question might not be obvious to him now, but how will he feel after the novelty fades and every day starts to feel the same? The movie *Groundhog Day* addresses that question. The main character, a cynical weatherman named Phil, is forced to live the same day over and over. At first, he finds joy in eating everything he wants without worrying about it since the next day will just reset with no ramifications. Eventually, though, his day lacks so much meaning that the despair causes him to try to take his life. Of course he is unsuccessful, since the day just resets itself again. In that movie, one of the reasons Phil is so depressed is because life provides little meaning if it is just an endless stream of random things.

We find entertainment enjoyable partly because it exists alongside other forms of activity. Watching a series, playing a game, or scrolling through videos can feel like a reward after a day spent solving problems, building something, or helping other people. The contrast between effort and relaxation is part of what makes leisure satisfying. When that contrast disappears, the experience begins to change in ways people rarely anticipate. The good news for Phil was that he learned to find meaning and be less self-centered, which reset the day and he became someone who found true meaning through changing his mindset.

Due to their hard work, people often fall into the mindset that they deserve to get lost in endless streaming. Their day might go by quickly, but they may notice that nothing moved forward or improved. Watching someone else's story unfold can be a nice break, but eventually, you begin to feel something pulling you back toward your own. Distraction only feels good until it doesn't.

One of the most interesting warnings about this kind of distraction appeared in a *Star Trek* episode. In 1991, during the fifth season of "Star Trek: The Next Generation," the writers produced an episode called "The Game." At the time, personal computers were still relatively new, the internet barely existed for most people, and smartphones were decades away. Yet the story imagined a device that behaved in a way that now feels surprisingly familiar.

In the episode, a visitor brings a small game device onto the Starship Enterprise. The device looks a bit like the kind of headset a singer might wear during a performance, except a small display sits in front of one eye. When someone puts it on, they see a simple game where they guide a glowing object onto a target. The game itself looks harmless. It is simple, satisfying, and easy to play. When the player succeeds, the device delivers a small burst of pleasure, much like the dopamine release people experience when something feels rewarding.

Crew members begin passing the device around so others can try it. At first, it seems like nothing more than entertainment. The game is quick and enjoyable, and people laugh as they experiment with it. Gradually, though, something strange begins to happen. Crew members start playing the game more often. People lose interest in work and even in conversation because they want to return to the device. Eventually, many of them spend most of their time using the game. They walk around the ship expressionless, as if they are somewhere else mentally.

The Enterprise crew slowly loses its ability to function because the game keeps rewarding them with small bursts of pleasure that make it difficult to stop. But the device was never designed to help people grow, build, or contribute. The device was designed as a secret weapon meant to take over the officers' minds and help an alien race conquer the Federation by hooking the crew onto the rush of dopamine.

When you watch that episode today, it feels almost prophetic. Phones, apps, games, and streaming platforms are incredibly good at keeping your attention locked onto the next piece of content. Each scroll, click, or episode gives your brain just enough stimulation to make continuing feel effortless. It feels harmless in the moment because nothing dramatic is happening. You are simply watching something interesting or amusing. Yet the systems behind many of these platforms are designed to hold attention for as long as possible.

Part of the reason these systems are so effective is that they make everything effortless. You do not have to think very hard, struggle through a problem, or invest much energy to stay engaged. In contrast, the experiences that usually leave you feeling satisfied at the end of the day tend to ask something from you. Learning a new skill takes patience and repetition. Writing something worthwhile takes reflection and effort. Improving at anything, whether it is a profession, a hobby, or even a relationship, usually requires time and attention. The activities that matter most in life often ask you to stretch a little. Endless streams of digital content remove that stretch and replace it with something far easier to continue, which is why it's so easy to stay there longer than you ever planned.

Over time, people tend to feel most alive when they can see their effort produced something real. That might involve solving a difficult problem, helping another person improve, creating something that did not exist before, or mastering a skill that once felt out of reach. Moments like that matter because they involve participation.

Scrolling through content rarely produces the same effect. You may absorb information or react to something you see, yet the activity itself usually does not create anything that carries forward into the rest of your day. If an occasional evening disappears into a show or a few hours pass while you scroll through interesting videos, that doesn't seem like a problem. Everyone enjoys entertainment. The problem starts when that pattern replaces your desire to do anything else.

Imagine waking up each morning with no responsibilities pushing you forward. Instead of building something, learning something, or working with other people toward a goal, you open your phone and begin scrolling. The next day begins the same way, and the day after that follows the same pattern. At first, it may feel relaxing because there is no pressure and no urgency, but after a while something begins to feel slightly off. Days start to blur together. You may have seen hundreds of videos or headlines, yet it becomes difficult to point to anything that you actually did with your time. Nothing was especially difficult, yet nothing felt especially meaningful. You've become Phil from *Groundhog Day*.

It's easy to blame technology, but technology itself is not the problem. The same tools that deliver endless entertainment can also help you learn a language, start a business, connect with people around the world, write a book, teach a class, mentor someone who needs guidance, or build something that improves the lives of others. The device in your hand can support growth just as easily as it can support distraction. That is one way our devices today differ from the one in *Star Trek*. Your phone and computer can either distract you or help you grow, depending on how you choose to use them.

It begins with noticing where you spend most of your time. If most of your attention flows toward activities that require curiosity, effort, and participation, your abilities expand and your sense of direction becomes stronger. If most of your attention drifts toward effortless content, days can feel busy while your deeper abilities remain unused.

In the *Star Trek* episode, the crew eventually realized what the game was doing to them. Once they understood how the device was manipulating their attention, they were able to disable it and regain control of the ship. The real question is whether you can recognize where technology pulls your attention away and where you can use it more intentionally to create meaning in your life.

The hours of your day will always be filled with something. If the structure of your work fades and fewer external demands dictate how your time must be spent, you will gradually become the person responsible for deciding what deserves your energy. Some people will use that freedom to learn, build, connect, and explore ideas that stretch their abilities. Others may drift toward endless streams of content that keep the mind stimulated but rarely deepens the sense that a day mattered. Which of these will you be?

When your attention moves toward things that challenge you, connect you with others, or allow you to build something meaningful, you can look back at the day and see that your effort produced something, even if it's small. When most of your time flows into endless streams of content, the experience may feel pleasant in the moment yet hollow when you look back on it later. You must ask yourself if you want to participate in life or simply observe it. If you are reading this book, I imagine you have already answered that question. Others may never ask that question because they are content simply letting the days pass by.

You can continue to grow even as technology becomes more powerful. Intelligent systems will continue to advance, automating tasks and removing effort from many parts of daily life. That progress will create enormous opportunity, yet it will also create a new responsibility. You will have more freedom than previous generations to decide how to use your time and what deserves your effort.

That shift raises another, deeper question. What happens when endless information, entertainment, and stimulation are not enough to make people feel satisfied with their lives? What kinds of experiences create the sense that time was used well and that your abilities contributed to something meaningful?

Those questions begin to point you toward what truly creates direction, purpose, and meaning in a life that is no longer organized primarily by work.

whether you can recognize [illegible] really [illegible] way and where you can [illegible] going [illegible] to [illegible] our [illegible] new [illegible]

The [illegible] of your day will always be filled with something [illegible] [illegible] your [illegible] and [illegible] external demands [illegible] how your time [illegible] particularly [illegible] the [illegible] of [illegible] what [illegible] some people will [illegible] to learn [illegible] and explore ideas that [illegible] the [illegible] [illegible] of [illegible] but [illegible] the [illegible]

When your [illegible] and [illegible] your [illegible] with [illegible] or allow [illegible] something [illegible] you [illegible] [illegible] and [illegible] [illegible] your [illegible] and [illegible] in [illegible] [illegible] in life [illegible] have already answered this question [illegible] that [illegible] because they [illegible] [illegible]

[illegible] to [illegible] [illegible] to advance [illegible] and [illegible] parts of daily life [illegible] will [illegible] [illegible] [illegible] [illegible] and [illegible]

[illegible] that [illegible] and [illegible] [illegible] what [illegible] and [illegible] your [illegible] [illegible] [illegible] [illegible] [illegible]

CHAPTER 6

What Is Adaptive Curiosity?

I recently spoke with a woman who had spent the last year and a half working toward a doctorate in education. She reached out because she felt stuck. Her mentor was not giving her the direction she expected, and she was beginning to question whether she was even on the right path. She wondered whether she should continue in education or move toward something like business. She asked for my opinion on which direction she should take.

Honestly, it was challenging to answer her. I could hear how much time and effort she had already invested, and I did not want to discourage her. At the same time, I could not ignore the question of what that degree would actually do for her when she finished it.

The connection between what you learn and what you end up doing no longer follows a straight line. You can do everything right and still feel unsure about where it leads, which creates the pressure so many people feel. There are more choices than ever, but less clarity about how those choices play out over time.

For a long time, people believed that if they chose the right path and stayed committed, things would unfold in a predictable way. That belief worked when change moved slowly.

Today, the pace of change has made that kind of certainty harder to depend on, and that is where a different way of thinking starts to matter, which is where adaptive curiosity comes in.

When asked how I define curiosity, I usually keep it simple. Curiosity is the desire to learn or explore something. It pulls you toward new ideas, helps you ask better questions, and keeps you open to information you might have missed. It is tied to growth in almost every way you can think of, whether that shows up in engagement, innovation, or how you perform in your work.

Adaptive curiosity builds on that, but it changes how you use it. It is not just about exploring something new. It is about what you do with what you discover while things are still unfolding, and it reflects your ability to keep moving, learning, and adjusting at the same time, even when you do not have a clear picture of where things are going.

That may sound subtle, but it changes how you approach almost every decision. Most people think that learning leads to clarity, and that clarity leads to action. You gather information first, feel confident about the direction, and then you move, which made sense when paths were stable.

Now, it often works in reverse, because you take a step, learn from it, adjust, and the clarity comes later. If you go back to the woman considering her doctorate, the question she asked was framed around choosing the right direction before she continued, which is how most people approach decisions when they want to know the outcome first.

A more useful way to approach it is to shift the question slightly. Instead of asking which path is right, you start asking what you can learn from where you are right now and how that might open additional options, which changes the pressure immediately.

Instead of feeling like one decision determines everything, you begin to see how each step gives you more information about what fits and what does not. You are still making progress, but you are not waiting for certainty before you move, and that is what makes curiosity adaptive.

You are still exploring, but also paying attention to what you are learning about yourself along the way. You begin to notice what holds your attention, what energizes you, and what starts to feel misaligned, and those signals become part of how you decide what to do next.

This is where many people get stuck. There are so many options available now and it is easy to feel overwhelmed. You can take courses, switch careers, build something on your own, or move in a completely different direction. When you are faced with that many possibilities, it is natural to want to be sure before you choose.

The problem is that waiting for that level of certainty can keep you from moving at all. Adaptive curiosity shifts your focus away from getting the decision perfect and toward learning through action, so you begin to treat each step as a way to gather information rather than as a final answer, and that is what starts to create direction over time.

Think about your own experience. You have probably had moments where you pursued something with a very specific outcome in mind, only to realize later that what you gained was useful in ways you had not expected. The value was not just in the result, but in what you learned along the way, and adaptive curiosity makes that process intentional.

Instead of looking back and realizing something was useful, you begin to move forward with the understanding that every experience has the potential to shape what comes next. You start paying attention while it is happening, not just after the fact.

Additionally, people underestimate the role of letting go. When you have invested time in a certain direction, it is easy to hold onto it longer than you should because you have built the experience and created an expectation for where it should lead. This is why changing direction can feel like losing something even when it is the right move.

You can see this in small ways. Anyone who has tried to change a golf swing after years of doing it one way knows how hard it is to adjust, because the old pattern is familiar even if it is no longer working. The same thing happens with bigger decisions.

Adaptive curiosity gives you a way to recognize when something no longer fits without feeling like you are starting over. The experience you have built does not disappear, but evolves, so you begin to see how it can apply in different ways instead of only in the way you originally expected.

That is exactly what the woman in that conversation needed. Getting her doctorate may still make sense or it may not, but what matters more is how she uses what she is learning while she is in it. The research skills, the ability to analyze information, and the discipline it takes to stay with a long-term goal can translate into multiple directions.

When you start to look at it that way, the decision is no longer about committing to one outcome. It becomes about expanding what is possible, and that shift also changes how you think about confidence.

Many people believe confidence comes from knowing what will happen, but in reality, it often comes from trusting that you can figure things out as they happen. It grows as you take steps, learn from them, and adjust based on what you discover.

You do not need to see the entire path to move forward. You need enough information to take the next step and the willingness to learn from it, which becomes even more important as technology continues to change how work and opportunity are structured.

You may not be able to predict what your field will look like or how your role will evolve, but you can stay engaged, keep learning, and adjust as things shift, which is what keeps you from feeling stuck.

If you go back to the original question, what should I do next, the answer is not found in trying to predict the future perfectly.

It comes from how you approach what is in front of you right now, using what you have, taking a step, and allowing that step to teach you something useful.

As you think about your own situation, notice where you may be waiting for clarity before you act and ask yourself what small step would give you better information than thinking about it longer, because that is how direction begins to take shape.

You move, you learn, you adjust, and over time those adjustments build something that feels far more aligned than anything you could have planned at the beginning, which is what adaptive curiosity allows you to do.

PART II

The Human Need for Meaning

CHAPTER 7

Why Information Is Not Enough

There is a big difference between people who watch sports and people who play them. You can see it in almost any stadium. One group sits in the stands talking about strategy, debating statistics, and analyzing every move the athletes make. The other group wakes up early to train, spends hours practicing, and deals with frustration, mistakes, and fatigue while they try to improve. Both groups may love the same sport, yet their experiences are completely different because one group observes while the other participates.

That contrast points to something important about how people experience life. Watching someone else accomplish something impressive can be entertaining and even inspiring, yet the experience changes dramatically when you step onto the field yourself and become part of the effort. Participation changes the emotional stakes of what you are doing because the progress, the struggle, and the outcome now belong to you rather than to someone you observe from a distance.

An inspiring example of someone who refused to remain on the sidelines is Erik Weihenmayer, whom I had the chance to interview on my radio show. Erik became the first blind person to reach the summit of Mount Everest. That achievement alone would be remarkable, yet Everest was only one chapter in a much larger story. Erik has climbed the Seven Summits, the highest peak on each continent, kayaked the entire length of the Grand Canyon, and taken on climbs that challenge even the most experienced adventurers.

When you hear about accomplishments like these, it is easy to focus only on the dramatic outcome and forget how many moments along the way could have convinced him to stop. Losing his sight might have given him every reason to step away from activities that require balance, navigation, and extraordinary endurance. Instead of retreating from those challenges, he chose to move toward them. He trained, learned new skills, built teams of people who supported his goals, and kept moving forward even when the path in front of him was uncertain.

What makes Erik's story powerful is not only what he accomplished, but the decision behind it. He chose to engage with life directly rather than treating it like something happening around him. That idea directly connects to the challenge many people face today. In a world filled with endless information about what other people are doing, it becomes surprisingly easy to stay in observer mode instead of stepping into the arena yourself. People read, watch, listen, and analyze, yet the transition from learning to actually doing becomes harder than it should be.

Years ago, most people did not have the option of studying something endlessly before trying it. If you wanted to learn how to do something, you usually had to jump in and start doing it. You experimented, made mistakes, adjusted, and gradually improved through experience because there were not thousands of videos, articles, and expert opinions waiting to be analyzed first. Today, the situation looks very different because information surrounds you almost constantly. Advice, tutorials, expert commentary, and opinions appear instantly whenever you search for them. You can learn almost anything online. You can study philosophy, understand how the brain works, or how to design a website. You can analyze financial markets, learn how to repair a car engine, or how to prepare an elaborate meal. Entire libraries now sit inside devices that fit comfortably in your pocket.

At first, that level of access sounds like a tremendous advantage. If knowledge opens doors, then unlimited knowledge should make it easier to decide what to do with your life. Many people assume that once they gather enough information, the right direction will become obvious.

What people actually experience tends to be far more complicated than they expect because information that first appears helpful can quickly turn into a flood of competing ideas that make it harder to decide what to do next.

Having access to enormous amounts of information does not automatically create clarity and, in many situations, produces the opposite effect because advice arrives from every direction, experts disagree with one another, strategies multiply, and the number of possible paths expands faster than anyone can realistically evaluate. When every option appears equally promising, even motivated and capable people can struggle to decide which direction deserves their attention.

You have probably experienced something like this in everyday life. You use your phone to look up a simple answer and suddenly find yourself reading article after article or watching video after video on the same topic. One expert recommends a method that sounds convincing, yet another suggests the exact opposite approach. A third introduces an entirely different perspective that also sounds reasonable. By the time you finish, you may understand the subject better than before, yet you still have no clear sense of what you should do with the information you just gathered.

One reason this pattern is so common is that the process often feels productive while it is happening, since you are learning, collecting ideas, and discovering new possibilities. Your brain receives small rewards each time you uncover something interesting, which creates the impression that progress is being made. Yet nothing in your life changes because learning about something and doing something are fundamentally different activities.

This pattern appears in many areas of modern life. People read books about entrepreneurship, listen to interviews with successful founders, and follow business leaders on social media. Others watch endless videos about fitness routines, cooking techniques, or creative hobbies. They gather strategies, frameworks, and advice from people who have mastered those skills. The information can be fascinating and often inspiring yet gathering knowledge does not automatically translate into action.

You may have experienced this yourself. You discover a topic that interests you and begin imagining what it would be like to become good at it. Perhaps you watch several videos about photography, woodworking, painting, writing, or learning a new language. For a while, you picture yourself developing that skill and enjoying the process. Days pass, then weeks, and the idea remains exactly where it started because learning about something and actually beginning it requires very different kinds of commitment.

I saw this pattern frequently when I worked as a doctoral chair helping students complete their doctoral degrees. One of the first steps in that process requires students to study a topic that interests them and identify a question that has not been fully answered. The goal is not to solve the largest problem in the field but to contribute something useful to an existing conversation.

Many students arrived with enormous collections of articles, notes, and research summaries. They understood the literature surrounding their topic extremely well and could explain every major study connected to it. The difficulty usually surfaced when it was time to move forward with their own contribution. Some students spent years preparing because they believed their work needed to be groundbreaking before it deserved to exist.

Others struggled because they had gathered so much information that they no longer knew where to begin. I saw students print stacks of articles that filled entire desks and filing cabinets. From the outside it looked like intense productivity, yet much of that activity was simply research without direction. The more information they gathered, the harder it became to decide what their own work should focus on.

Eventually, many of them reached an important realization that changed how they approached the process. A dissertation does not need to cure cancer or solve the most important problem in the world; it simply needs to add something to the existing field of thought. Once students accepted that idea and began writing, progress accelerated quickly because they already possessed the knowledge required. The real barrier was not a lack of information; it was hesitation.

That hesitation takes many different forms, sometimes growing out of perfectionism, sometimes tied to fear of criticism, and for many people, appearing as endless preparation that never quite turns into action. Regardless of how it shows up, the outcome tends to look the same, because people remain in the planning phase far longer than necessary and delay the moment when they must begin.

Living in a world full of information can reinforce that habit because it is always possible to find one more article, one more podcast, or one more expert opinion before making a decision. The search for certainty begins to replace the willingness to experiment.

You can see the effect of information overload in smaller decisions as well. When too many options compete for your attention at the same time, the brain begins to slow down instead of speeding up. Instead of helping you choose, the abundance of possibilities creates hesitation because each option requires comparison, evaluation, and second-guessing. The more alternatives appear, the easier it becomes for you to postpone the decision altogether.

That same pattern appears when people begin thinking about what they should do with their lives. When the path in front of you feels obvious, moving forward feels natural. When dozens of possibilities compete for your attention, choosing one can feel far more difficult than expected.

This is where adaptive curiosity becomes important. Adaptive curiosity is different from casual interest because it pushes you to keep adjusting your thinking as you learn. It often begins with a simple question that keeps returning to your mind. You start wondering how something works, why certain patterns repeat, or what might happen if you explored an idea more deeply. At first, that curiosity may lead you toward books, conversations, and articles that help you understand the subject better, yet its real value appears when it encourages you to keep adapting your approach as you experiment and learn through experience.

Think about something you eventually learned how to do well. It might have been a professional skill, a sport, a musical instrument, or a hobby that gradually became meaningful to you. At some point, you probably gathered information that explained the basics. That knowledge helped you begin, yet your deeper understanding developed only after you started practicing.

Your earlier attempts probably do not look impressive. That is part of the process because real skill develops through repetition, adjustment, and patience as your brain and body gradually adapt to the work. What once felt awkward slowly becomes familiar, and your competence grows through actual participation rather than through observation.

The same principle applies when people search for direction in their lives. Reading about purpose or success can be interesting and even motivating, yet those ideas can remain abstract until you begin exploring them through real experiences.

That might entail that you volunteer for a project, begin learning a new skill, join a group centered around something that interests you, or help someone who could benefit from your experience. As you try different things, you start noticing what energizes you and what does not. Those signals often reveal far more about your direction than reading about possibilities ever could.

Technology will continue expanding your access to knowledge, which means information will become even easier to obtain than it is today. The real difference between people who find meaning and those who don't will increasingly depend on what they choose to do with that knowledge once they have it.

Some of you will continue gathering ideas, reading more articles, watching more videos, and studying more strategies without ever moving past preparation without follow-through. There are those of you who will treat information as a starting point and begin experimenting. You will test ideas, build projects, learn from mistakes, and gradually shape your lives through participation rather than observation.

Adaptive curiosity pushes you to move beyond collecting information and toward trying something with it. Instead of asking what else you need to know, the question shifts to what you are willing to attempt. The direction you should attempt rarely appears while you are sitting on the sidelines studying possibilities. It begins to emerge once you step into the game and start learning through experience.

Think again about the difference between the sports fan and the athlete. Both may understand the rules of the game, yet only one feels the pressure of the moment, the frustration of mistakes, and the satisfaction that comes from improving through effort.

There used to be a line on ABC's Wide World of Sports: "The thrill of victory and the agony of defeat." Life offers the same choice. You can spend your time watching remarkable stories unfold around you, or you can step onto the field and begin creating your own. If you stay on the sidelines, you may avoid the agony of defeat, but you will never experience the thrill of victory, either.

CHAPTER 8

The Importance of Contribution

If you have ever spent time around a sales team, you have probably seen some version of the small ceremony that happens when someone closes a deal. Every office seems to have its own way of celebrating. In one company I remember, the salesperson walked across the room, grabbed a rope attached to a brass bell, and pulled it hard enough for the entire floor to hear. Heads would lift from behind computer screens, people would clap or cheer for a moment, and then everyone would return to what they were doing. In another office, the signal sounded completely different because the moment a deal came through, music played through the speakers. Each salesperson had a different song, so everyone instantly knew who had made the sale. No matter how it was done, it always felt the same. For a few moments the energy in the room lifted, people smiled, and then everyone's attention shifted right back to finding the next big sales opportunity.

There is nothing wrong with enjoying that kind of recognition. It feels good to have your effort acknowledged, even briefly. You walk back to your desk with the sense that something you did mattered, and for a short time the entire environment feels lighter. The problem is how quickly it fades. Anyone who has worked in that kind of setting knows how fast the focus shifts. Within minutes, the phones ring again, screens fill with new tasks, and the moment becomes part of the past. The phrase that gets repeated in those sales environments captures it perfectly: You are only as good as your last deal.

You have likely experienced another kind of moment that feels like this. It may not come with applause or music, and no one may even notice it when it happens. It might be at the end of a long day when you realize that something you did helped another person move forward in a meaningful way. You may have helped a colleague solve a problem that had been frustrating them for weeks or shared something you learned the hard way so someone else could avoid making the same mistake. Even simpler, you listened when someone needed encouragement more than advice and later discovered that the conversation meant far more to them than you expected. When experiences like that happen, the feeling stays with you. It lingers in a way that recognition rarely does, because you know your effort made a difference.

Most people don't need a long explanation to recognize the difference between a moment that feels good for a second and one that lingers. For years, that second kind of feeling was simply part of how work felt, and most people did not stop to question it because it seemed so natural. A teacher would see a student finally understand something that had been frustrating them. A nurse would walk out of a room knowing someone trusted them at a time when that trust really mattered. There were people building things, fixing problems, guiding others, or simply helping in ways that made life a little better for someone else, even if no one stopped to call attention to it.

For many, that sense of connection isn't as easy to see. Work looks different than it used to. Technology takes care of things that once required entire teams, and people move between roles more often, sometimes stepping away from traditional jobs earlier than they expected or creating paths that don't resemble anything they originally planned. When that structure starts to shift, those small signals that once made it obvious your effort mattered don't always appear in the same way. When that happens, it's natural to wonder if a title or role no longer gives you that sense of purpose. Where does purpose come from?

I have thought about this many times, partly because I grew up watching someone who answered it in a powerful way. My uncle was D. Ralph Millard, M.D. He wasn't actually my uncle, but my second cousin, and I came from a family where you were taught never to call your elders by their first name. So, my second cousin was referred to as my uncle Ralph, who became one of the most influential plastic surgeons in the world because of his work repairing cleft lips and palates. On paper, he had every reason to focus entirely on building a prestigious and financially successful medical career concentrating on cosmetic procedures and private patients.

Yet the work that mattered most to him had very little to do with prestige or financial success. Early in his career he developed a groundbreaking technique for repairing cleft lips. The procedure dramatically improved the way surgeons could restore the natural shape of a child's lip and face. For children born with cleft deformities, that change affected far more than appearance. It influenced how easily they could eat, how clearly they could speak, and how confidently they could interact with the people around them.

Once my uncle recognized the difference that technique could make, he began traveling to places where children had little or no access to reconstructive surgery. Many families in those regions could never afford specialized care, and some of the children had spent years hiding their faces because of how others responded to them. My uncle volunteered his time performing surgeries that allowed those children to smile, speak, and move through the world without the constant stigma they had experienced before treatment.

Those trips did not bring large financial rewards or widespread recognition, yet they were the experiences he spoke about with the most enthusiasm. His work led to the creation of the D. Ralph Millard society, and my husband and I were fortunate to attend one of those society dinners where his residents clearly respected the contribution he made to the world.

He could have spent every hour building a lucrative medical practice, yet the stories that stayed with him were the ones where he saw a child look in a mirror after surgery and realize that life might be different from that moment forward.

You and I may never become surgeons, yet the lesson behind that story has little to do with medicine. The experiences that stay with you rarely revolve around titles, status, or applause. They tend to involve helping another person move forward in a meaningful way.

You can see this same pattern in everyday life. You have probably had moments where you knew you made a difference. Think about a time when you helped someone see a solution they had not noticed, or when you shared an idea that made their path easier. Even a small moment of encouragement can change how someone approaches a challenge. Those moments tend to stay with you because they carry a sense of meaning that is hard to ignore.

As the world continues to change, this idea becomes even more important. Earlier, we explored how identity has often been tied to occupation. When someone asks what you do, your answer has traditionally provided a quick way to understand where you fit. But as traditional career paths have evolved, many people began searching for other ways to answer that deeper question of where they belong.

Contribution started to fill that space because it is less focused on the title you hold than the value you create. Someone who mentors others may never appear on an organizational chart, yet their influence can shape many lives. A person who volunteers regularly may never receive a promotion, yet their effort may improve an entire community over time.

When you begin looking at life through the lens of how you can contribute, the questions you ask yourself start to change. Instead of focusing only on position or recognition, you begin noticing where your knowledge, experience, or perspective might help someone else move forward. That shift changes how you evaluate both your work and your life.

A conversation I once had on my radio show with Scott Harrison illustrates how that shift can happen. Scott began his career as a nightclub promoter in New York City, a role built around entertainment, energy, and social status. From the outside, his life looked very exciting, but over time, he realized it left him feeling empty.

During a period when he was trying to figure out what direction his life should take, he volunteered on a hospital ship that provided medical care in regions where healthcare was extremely limited. Many of the illnesses he treated were connected to unsafe drinking water. Entire communities struggled with problems that could have been prevented if clean water had been available.

That observation stayed with him long after he returned home. Instead of moving on, he kept thinking about what he had seen and what could be done about it. That curiosity eventually led him to create the company Charity: Water, an organization that builds clean water systems in communities that need them. Over time, the organization would help bring safe water to millions of people around the world.

Scott did not begin his career planning to build a global nonprofit. The direction emerged because he paid attention to a problem that affected real people and chose to respond to it. Once he saw the difference that work could make, the effort felt meaningful in a way his earlier career never had.

This is where someone like Scott used adaptive curiosity in a way that created real value for other people. He paid attention to problems, patterns, and possibilities that others overlooked. Approaching things this way keeps you engaged with what is happening around you and pushes you to explore how things could be better. When curiosity connects with contribution, learning begins to serve a purpose that extends beyond personal interest.

When you develop this kind of thinking, what feels like just another hour on the calendar begins to feel more worthwhile because you can see where your effort is going. The work does not suddenly become easy, and it still takes patience and follow-through, but it no longer feels like you are just filling time; it feels like you are doing something that matters.

Most of the time, the sense that you are contributing does not come from one big moment that stands out on its own. It builds slowly and is easy to overlook if you are not paying attention. Someone who invests in helping others grow may end up shaping careers without ever setting out to do that. A parent who encourages curiosity may influence how their children think long after their children are grown. A mentor who offers guidance may help someone gain the confidence they did not realize they could have.

When you start looking at life this way, it becomes hard not to notice how many opportunities there are to contribute. They are not limited to a job or title, and they do not require a big stage to matter. They are there in everyday situations, in conversations, in relationships, and in moments when someone simply needs help, guidance, or encouragement. These moments are easy to miss if you are not paying attention, and easy to pass up if you assume they are not important enough to matter.

Adaptive curiosity helps you notice those openings because it keeps your attention focused on possibilities rather than limitations. When you remain curious about the people and situations around you, you begin to see where your effort might create value.

As this perspective develops, recognition begins to follow your contributions rather than the other way around. In earlier systems, recognition often came from titles, promotions, or formal authority. In a world where those structures continue to shift, recognition increasingly grows from the value people experience through your actions and the difference you make in their lives.

That shift leads naturally to another question: When titles and positions no longer define status in the same way, what determines how people earn respect and influence in a world that values contribution more than hierarchy?

CHAPTER 9

Recognition Without Titles

I have worked with a lot of leaders and a surprising number of them have an insecurity that they hesitate to share with anyone. In leadership circles, they call it imposter syndrome. Those with the experience, the accomplishments, and the recognition can still find themselves wondering if they really deserve their title. It can hold people back from taking opportunities they would likely do well in, because they do not want to feel exposed. Women are more likely to turn down opportunities if they do not feel they meet every requirement.

You have probably heard someone talk about what they have built or the title they hold, and before you even realize it, you start measuring yourself against them. You might wonder how they got there, how long it took, or why it seems like they moved faster than you. Even when you are doing well, that comparison can make you question yourself in a way that does not match the reality of your abilities.

I remember feeling that sense of comparison the first time I walked into a board of advisors meeting at Docusign. I was honored to be included on that board and as I looked around the room, I saw people who had built companies most of us only read about, leaders from major organizations, and individuals whose names I had heard before, which made them feel hard to relate to at first. Whether they came from a Fortune 100 company, had led NASA, or were known from shows like *Shark Tank*, it was an impressive group. It was hard not to ask myself how I ended up there.

The reason I had been invited was because I had interviewed Keith Krach, who was the CEO of Docusign at the time, and he saw something a lot of people overlook. He knew that putting people in a room with different experiences, different backgrounds, and different ways of thinking leads to better ideas. He wasn't looking for people with the same résumé. He was looking for people who could add unique insights.

Once everyone began interacting and sharing feedback, it became much clearer to me why each person was there, regardless of what their title was. People listened, asked thoughtful questions, and challenged ideas when it made sense. No one was comparing titles or trying to stand out. They were there to contribute, and that made the entire experience feel completely different from what I had initially expected when walking into the room.

That experience changed how I thought about my own value. I was not there because of a title. I was there because I brought something to the conversation, even if it was not obvious to me at first. That is easy to forget when you compare yourself to what you think someone else's title represents, especially when you are filling in the blanks about their success.

Sometimes it is hard to see your own value when you are constantly looking at what everyone else is doing. Social media has made that even harder. You might feel good about your work, and then you scroll for a few minutes and see someone announce a promotion or a big milestone, and suddenly you start questioning yourself. You can be happy for them and still wonder if you should be doing something different or moving faster, and that can chip away at your confidence if you are not careful.

The problem is comparing your full experience to what someone else chooses to show. People do not post the parts that did not go well, the doubts, or the mistakes. You see a very edited version of their life and use that to judge your own, which is never a fair comparison.

At the same time, there is another kind of pressure that pushes people in a completely different way. You hear "fake it until you make it" so often that it starts to sound like a rule instead of a suggestion. It creates this sense that you need to look more established than you really are just to be taken seriously. The trouble is, once you start doing that, it pulls your attention away from what you are building. You spend more energy managing how things appear than improving what is real, and over time that gap becomes harder to ignore.

You can see how far that can go when it gets out of control. Theranos, a company that claimed to have a breakthrough blood-testing technology that never actually worked, is an extreme example of what can happen when the need to appear successful takes over. Most people would never go as far as Theranos founder Elizabeth Holmes did, but the pressure behind it is something many people recognize in smaller ways.

When I interviewed Bethany McLean, whose work exposed what happened at Enron, one of the most well-known corporate fraud scandals in history, she told me she believed people do not always set out to mislead others. In many cases, they begin believing the version of the story they have been telling. Over time, that can make it harder to recognize what is real, and that gap grows slowly, doing too much damage before anyone realizes it.

I have seen incredibly capable people feel like they need to exaggerate their experience just to get attention. It is like a puffer fish trying to look bigger than it is, not because it wants to deceive, but because it feels like it must to compete. That reaction does not come from arrogance. It usually comes from feeling that just being good at something is not enough to stand out.

If you think about both experiences for a minute, the self-doubt from experiencing imposter syndrome and the pressure to look more accomplished are tied together. They both come from how you measure yourself and how you assume others are measuring you, even when those assumptions aren't accurate.

For a long time, titles made this simple. If someone moved into a bigger role, you understood what that meant without thinking about it, as you had a clear sense of where you stood and what moving forward looked like.

That doesn't feel the same anymore. You can stay busy all day, work hard, and still end the day wondering if any of it is really getting you where you want to go. When you don't have those clear signals, it's easy to start questioning yourself and wondering if you are on the right track.

Comparison doesn't disappear. It just becomes harder to read. Instead of focusing only on titles, you start noticing who people listen to, who influences decisions, and who others turn to when something matters.

There is another layer to this that people are starting to feel but may not fully have words for yet. The future of work is not as stable as it once was. Roles are changing, industries are shifting, and many of the jobs people once relied on will look very different or even disappear. That can feel unsettling, especially if you have spent years working toward a certain title only to realize the path itself may not stay the same.

Technology is a big part of that shift. Things that once took years to learn can now be done much faster, and far more people can do them. When that happens, titles stop giving you a clear picture of who is adding value.

When that starts to happen, your attention naturally moves toward something more practical. You care less about what someone is called and more about what they actually do when things get complicated. You notice who can take something messy and make sense of it, who can explain something clearly, and who can help move things forward when others feel stuck. That kind of contribution stands out because it helps, and that matters more than any label.

It is sometimes easy to miss those moments already happening in your own life. Think about when someone asks for your opinion, includes you in a conversation that matters, or turns to you when they need help figuring something out. Those moments say a lot about how people see you, even if no one ever puts a label on it.

Those interactions do not always feel special when they happen, yet they often reveal far more about your value than any title ever could. When you start paying attention to those moments, you realize that progress does not come from a title or promotion. You can see it in how people trust you, how they include you, and how you make a difference, even in ways that may have felt small before but add up over time.

Adaptive curiosity helps you catch the moments when your input helps drive a conversation, or when people rely on you to make sense of something that isn't clear. Those moments say a lot about the value you bring.

When you begin to see that, you recognize that you do not need a label to tell you whether you're doing well. This also takes some of the pressure out of comparison. You may still notice what others are doing, but it doesn't hit the same way because you have a clearer sense of your own direction.

This matters even more as work continues to change. When more people can do similar tasks, titles stop being the main way to stand out. What matters is how you think, how you handle uncertainty, and how you help things progress when there isn't a clear path.

When you focus on that, you spend less time worrying about how things look and more time putting your energy into work that challenges you and keeps you interested. You notice where you're making a difference because you can feel it in the way others respond.

From there, the question becomes how you choose to spend your time and where you focus your attention, and what you decide is worth your effort when no one is laying out a plan for you. That is where your direction begins to take shape.

CHAPTER 10

Participation as the New Signal

Over the course of the many years my show ran, I was fortunate to interview some of the most interesting people of our time. Whether I spoke with experts on negotiation, influence, or making an impact, they all touched on the value of participation. One of the reasons I was inspired to write about curiosity was seeing the difference these people made. They could have easily sat back and watched life unfold, but they chose to participate and make a difference.

As we witness the world dramatically change due to intelligent machines, we wonder what the future will look like. Even the people who work with technology every day cannot say for sure what is coming next, and that uncertainty is unsettling. You might wonder what will happen to the value of everything you have learned and your experience.

Many of you who have already been displaced by technology try to stay busy, but you might still feel like something is missing. You can fill your day and even check things off a to-do list and still have a nagging feeling that what you are doing every day does not really matter.

It should feel easier to know what to do, but the problem is there are so many choices. You are likely experiencing information overload. There are more ways than ever to stay busy doing things, but much of it can feel like it does not really make a difference or move you toward that feeling of finding your purpose. If you are not experiencing real participation in a way that feels like you added something meaningful, it may feel empty.

People do not miss opportunities to participate in a meaningful way because they do not care or are unwilling; it is because they are not seeing what others are seeing.

When I was doing research for my book, *The Power of Perception*, I interviewed Beau Lotto, a neuroscientist who studies how people make sense of what they see. What he explained helped me understand why people can look at the same situation and come away with completely different ideas about what matters. We are not reacting to reality; we are reacting to what we think it is based on.

Your brain filters constantly. It looks for things that match what it expects and ignores anything that does not. That means two people can be looking at the same situation and one immediately sees what is missing or what needs to change, while the other sees nothing wrong. These people can be equally capable but notice different things.

You have probably seen this in the well-known experiment, the Invisible Gorilla conducted by Christopher Chabris and Daniel Simons, where people are asked to watch a group passing a basketball and count the passes. In the middle of that, a person in a gorilla suit walks right through the scene, and a surprising number of people never see it. They are not careless or distracted. They are simply focused on what they were told to look for, so everything else gets filtered out. The same thing happens in everyday situations, which is why some opportunities are obvious to one person and invisible to another.

I have worked with people who seem to be very intuitive about how to fix things, what is missing in a situation, and why something needs to be changed. They walk into a room and quickly see connections or gaps that others overlook. At the same time, I have seen people look at the exact same situation and think everything is fine, even when there are clear opportunities to improve something. That difference often comes down to perception.

Some of you will choose not to participate, not because you do not see the value in it, but because you are not sure where to start.

Participation includes recognizing where you could contribute and doing something with what you see. Many people get stuck because seeing something and acting on it are two different steps.

There have been times when you probably noticed something small that did not make sense and didn't do anything about it. It might have been something inefficient, something missing, or something that could have been improved, and you told yourself it was not your place or not worth the effort. Later, you saw someone else point out the exact same thing and act on it, and you realize you should have done more. The difference was never your ability, but whether you decided to act on what you saw.

When you begin to understand how perception shapes what you notice, it becomes easier to see why participation looks so different from one person to another.

To become someone who participates in a meaningful way, you must learn to interrupt that pattern. That usually happens when you pay attention to things that do not quite make sense or when you spend more time on something instead of moving on right away. When that happens, you notice what you have been missing, and once you notice it, you have a choice about what to do next.

Learning to participate more can make your life more meaningful. If you continue to pass on opportunities to participate, those who notice more and act will stand out.

You likely already know that when something matters to you, you put more effort in and are more open to trying. The problem is, when there is no clear path, it is easy to wait and assume someone will tell you how to participate. Without this structure, you must decide what you will participate in and to what extent. The longer you wait, the easier it gets to keep waiting and feel stuck. When that happens, you must be willing to start participating anyway, even in small ways.

This can start with sharing an idea, helping someone, or trying something you have been thinking about for a while. Over time, those actions begin to change how you see yourself and what you believe is possible. At some point, it becomes clear that you do not need the perfect role or the right conditions to contribute. You only need to decide that what you know and what you can do is worth something, and the real question is whether you are willing to look a little closer.

CHAPTER 11

How Meaning Actually Forms

You likely have a few memories from your childhood that stand out more clearly than the rest. For me, I can remember being very young, sitting with my entire family in front of our television, watching Apollo 11 land on the moon. It felt like the whole world sat in silent awe, because in that moment, Buzz Aldrin and his fellow astronauts had just done something no human being had ever done before. From that moment on, he became one of the most recognized people on the planet.

What Aldrin experienced after that life-changing moment may surprise you. He has spoken openly about falling into depression and struggling with alcohol in the years after the mission. When the clear goal shaping his days disappeared almost overnight, and the structure guiding his life was gone, there was no next mission that could compare. What replaced it was something far less defined and much harder to deal with, which was trying to figure out what gave his life direction after the one thing that seemed like it should have answered that was already behind him.

Moments like these, that you would expect would define you, can actually force you to reconsider the meaning in your own life. Most people assume that achieving something big enough will finally settle the feeling they are chasing.

Aldrin's experience tells you that a moment can be extraordinary, but the feeling does not linger the way people expect it to. The achievement ends, the attention fades, and you are left trying to make sense of your life without that goal driving you.

What makes this even more interesting is that not everyone responded the same way. Neil Armstrong, who took that first step onto the moon, handled things very differently. He stepped away from the spotlight, focused on teaching, and spoke very little about the mission as something that defined him. When he did talk about how he approached life, he emphasized curiosity, problem solving, and continuing to work on things that interested him. He stayed focused on what was ahead of him instead of what he had already done.

That is where you start to see the difference. Meaning is not tied to the size of an achievement. It comes from what you do with your life once the moment has passed.

You do not need to walk on the moon to see this pattern. Think about the last time you reached something you had been working toward for a long time. It might have been a promotion, finishing a degree, closing a deal, or even something personal you had been trying to accomplish. There is a moment right after where you feel good about it. You should. You earned it. Then a little time passes, and something changes. The feeling settles, and you realize it did not fill what you thought it would.

I hear this all the time from people. Someone will tell me they finally reached a goal they had been chasing for years, and almost immediately, they follow it with a question about what they should do now. It is not that they are ungrateful. It is that the moment did not answer the question in the way they thought it would.

That is where people tend to get stuck. Instead of sitting with that realization, many assume the answer is to pursue something bigger. They raise the stakes and set a new goal, believing the next one will feel different. For a while it might, but the pattern usually repeats itself. The satisfaction fades faster than expected, and they must address that question all over again: Now what?

You probably know that meaning does not come from a single moment. It builds through the kinds of experiences you have and how connected you feel to them while you are in them. You can find meaning in ways that are easy to dismiss because they do not look significant when you compare them to the larger milestones you have been taught to value.

You might not think of it as meaning at the time, but it comes when you are absorbed in something and lose track of time, or when you help someone in a way that matters to them. You might feel it when you create something and recognize that it comes from your effort.

Most people have had those moments, yet they tend to overlook them because they are focused on something bigger. When that happens, they begin chasing meaning in places that are easier to see but less likely to give them what they are looking for.

This can create a gap between what you are doing and how you feel about what you have accomplished. Even when you stay busy and accomplish things, you can still feel disconnected from your own life. That disconnect comes from how involved you feel in what you are doing, not from how many things you accomplish.

You may start to notice your sense of involvement fading as your days turn into routines and habits. You might feel like you are on autopilot, completing tasks without feeling particularly connected to them. When that becomes normal, even experiences that could feel meaningful pass by without leaving much of an impression.

Another pattern that keeps you from meaningful experiences is waiting to have clarity before you act. It feels reasonable to want to know what will be meaningful before you invest your time in it. The problem is that clarity usually comes from experience, not from thinking about it in advance. When you wait until everything makes sense, you delay the very experiences that would have helped you figure it out.

There is also pressure to stay with the way you have defined yourself in the past. When you have spent years building a certain version of your life, changing direction can feel uncomfortable. It can feel like you are stepping away from something that once mattered, even when you know it no longer fits the way it used to.

If you step back and look at what creates a sense of meaning, you find it when you are involved in what you are doing, when your effort matters to someone or something beyond you, and when your time is spent in a way that feels worthwhile.

When those elements are present, people tend to feel connected to their lives, but when they are missing, something feels off, even if everything looks fine from the outside.

That realization can be uncomfortable because it forces you to examine what you have been prioritizing. You may start to notice that some of the things you worked hardest to achieve did not give you the feeling you expected.

Once you see that pattern, you stop asking what will look successful and begin asking what will actually feel worth it. This changes how you pay attention to your life. You start noticing what holds your interest, what pulls you in, and where your energy naturally goes when you are not forcing it. You begin to recognize that meaning is not something you arrive at; it is something that is built based on what you spend your time on and how connected you feel to it.

Aldrin reached an extraordinary moment and then had to figure out his life after it. Armstrong kept himself engaged in what he was learning, building, and working on. This is where people either keep building something meaningful or start feeling like something is missing.

PART III

Why Reinvention Is Difficult (FATE)

CHAPTER 12

Fear

When I wrote *Cracking the Curiosity Code*, I focused on the value of improving curiosity, which requires recognizing what inhibited it. That led me to create the Curiosity Code Index®, also referred to as the CCI, which identifies the main inhibitors of curiosity. After the popularity of that book, people kept asking me how to build a culture of curiosity at work. They also wanted to know more about the connection between curiosity and things like engagement, innovation, and other productivity-related factors, which I explained when I wrote *Curiosity Unleashed*. This book, *Adaptive Curiosity*, focuses on the value of using curiosity to adapt and explores how to find meaning in a world where guiding structures have been replaced by intelligent machines.

As I mentioned in a previous chapter, there are four things that can get in the way of curiosity. This and the next three chapters explain those inhibitors, which include fear, assumptions, technology, and environment.

When I first began studying curiosity, I wanted to understand what really impacted people's curiosity levels. After all, we begin as very curious children before something changes, and I wanted to know what that was.

Since my first book about curiosity was meant for businesspeople, I put a question out on LinkedIn and asked people what kept them from asking questions in meetings. I expected a range of answers, but the responses were overwhelmingly fear-based. So many comments leaned that way that I began to think fear might be the main inhibitor. When the results from my later research came in, all four inhibitors were almost equally problematic for people. Fear, however, was one of the first things people recognized.

What people described was something very common. They talked about sitting in meetings, thinking about a question, and deciding not to ask it because they assumed everyone else already knew the answer, and they did not want to look like they did not know something. That hesitation is common for many of us. We might not think it is a big deal at the time, but when you hold back in that way, it changes what you can learn and contributing, which ultimately impacts how you grow over time.

Most of us have had experiences working with people who inadvertently create fear in us. I know I have. When I speak with groups, I often share a story of a leader I worked with who asked me to do something I had never done before. I told him I would be happy to take it on, but I had never done it and wanted to understand how to approach it. He looked at me and said, "I'm going to pretend I didn't hear that." I assumed his response meant that by that point in my career, I should have known how to do that task. The reality was, there was never any reason for me to have done it before, as that skill was never built into any training. In addition to the not-so-subtle message that he saw me as incompetent, he also sent a clear message that asking questions was not encouraged. Fortunately for me, I was older at that time and less likely to be intimidated by that kind of behavior. But, if someone had treated me like that when I was younger, I'm sure it would have upset me.

He wasn't trying to be difficult. He was trained to talk like that because his boss likely treated him that way. A negative corporate culture flows downhill and experiences like that impact more than just that single interaction. They influence how people approach situations from that point forward.

If you bring that way of thinking into your job, you start to think twice before speaking up and rely on what you already know because it feels safer. Over time, that can limit how willing you are to explore new opportunities.

That same reaction is especially important right now. Many people are expected to learn new tools, explore new ideas, and contribute in ways that are not always clearly defined. If the response to uncertainty is to stay quiet or avoid asking questions, it becomes much harder to adapt. If you want to grow, you must be willing to try things even when you do not have everything figured out.

We all face different forms of fear, especially in a world where intelligent machines are changing what it means to contribute. You might feel like you are already behind, like others know something you do not, or like the abilities you spent years acquiring may not matter in the same way. You might hesitate because you do not want to look inexperienced while learning something new, or because you are not sure the time you invest will lead to something meaningful.

The problem is not that fear exists – it's that fear starts making decisions for you. When you are afraid, you stop asking questions you would normally ask, you avoid trying things, and you tell yourself that waiting makes more sense. Waiting can feel reasonable in the moment, but it often keeps you in the same place while everything around you continues to change.

Much of what you are feeling is tied to how you interpret what is happening. When you see others using tools or talking about ideas that feel unfamiliar, it is easy to assume they understand far more than you do, but most people are learning as they go. The difference is not that they have everything figured out. It is that they started interacting with something sooner, even in a small way, and built from there. Over time, that interaction becomes familiarity, and familiarity reduces fear.

Fear also affects how you see yourself. If you are used to being competent, it can feel uncomfortable to try something new where you must reinvent yourself. That discomfort can keep you from participating at all, but being new at something is not a sign that something is wrong. It is a sign that you are stretching into something that has the potential to expand what you can do. The longer you wait to begin, the longer you feel that discomfort.

Fear can also make you hesitate because you want to choose the right move before taking any step. You might tell yourself that you will start once you understand something better or once you know what the best option is. In periods of rapid change like we have today, that clarity usually comes after you take action, and not before. When you begin something new, even in a small way, you gain information that was not available to you before you started.

Past experiences can add another layer to this. If you struggled with something before or had an experience where you felt embarrassed or unsuccessful, it can influence how you approach something new. Instead of seeing a new situation for what it is, it can be a reminder of something that happened before. That can make your hesitation feel justified, even when the current situation is different than what you remembered. When you take a moment to look at what has changed, including what you know now and what resources are available to you, it becomes easier to see that you are not starting from the same place.

Fear often grows when everything feels overwhelming, especially when so much is changing. When the future feels uncertain, it helps to focus on what you can do next, because even small changes can make the situation more manageable, one thing at a time. This helps shift your thinking from worrying about change to doing something to adapt to it.

You can start by noticing where fear influences your decisions. Pay attention to the moments when you tell yourself that you are not ready, that you do not know enough, or that you will get to it later. Those are often signals that fear is guiding your choices. When you notice that, you have an opportunity to choose something different.

Instead of trying to solve everything at once, pick one thing you have been putting off and do something small about it. If technology feels overwhelming, explore one tool for one purpose. If you are concerned about relevance, look at the abilities you already have and consider how they might be used in a different way. If you are unsure where to begin, start with a question that helps you understand something you have been avoiding. These steps may seem small, but they start to change how you think about what you can do.

As you begin to act, even in small ways, you start to build evidence that you can adapt. That evidence matters because it changes how you see yourself. Instead of defining yourself only by what you already know, you begin to see yourself as someone who can learn, adjust, and contribute in new ways. Only then can you stop thinking in terms of what you already know and begin thinking in terms of what you can still learn, build, contribute, and become.

Focusing on overcoming your fears is one of the most important steps you can take to build adaptive curiosity. Once you understand how fear affects your decisions, it becomes much easier to recognize the other forces that have been limiting your curiosity as well.

In my research, I have found that fear is only one of four factors that impact curiosity, along with assumptions, technology, and environment. Together they form the acronym FATE. When these factors take hold, it can feel like life is happening to you instead of being influenced by you. That is why I designed the CCI, to help you discover what has been holding you back. If you want a deeper look at how those factors are affecting you personally, you can take the assessment at curiositycode.com.

CHAPTER 13

Assumptions

You make decisions every day about what you like, what you do not like, what you are good at, what you are not good at, and what is worth your time. Most of those decisions feel automatic, almost like common sense, and you rarely ask where they come from. They can feel helpful, like they are saving you time and keeping you focused on what matters, but many of those decisions are made before you have enough information, and this is how assumptions impact you far more than you realize.

When I talk about the impact of assumptions in my keynotes, I often hold up a bottle of water and ask a simple question, "How heavy is this?" People usually give a quick answer. Some yell out, 16 ounces, or some say 10, but all their answers are based on the weight of the bottle. I then explain that it is not about the weight, but about how long I hold it for. If I hold it for a minute, it's no big deal. If I hold it for an hour, my arm starts to get tired. If I hold it all day, it becomes more intolerable. The weight of the bottle never changes, but the experience of holding it does. What matters is not just what something is, but how long you carry it. This is how assumptions work – the longer you hold onto them, the more they cause discomfort.

Unlike fear, assumptions are not the first thing you think of as inhibiting you, but they have just as much of an influence on your behavior. Think of assumptions as that voice in your head that immediately reacts and tells you what you should like to do, consider doing, or avoid doing.

Your decisions are shaped by that voice, which comes from many places. Maybe you tried something once or twice and decided you didn't enjoy it or you weren't good at it, and your assumptions tell you whether you should even consider trying it again. Over time, your assumptions determine what you pay attention to and what you ignore. Drawing conclusions is a natural part of how we all learn. The problem is how early we form conclusions and how rarely we go back to question them.

If fear can stop you from starting, assumptions often decide whether something is even worth considering, which can keep you from trying at all.

People often close their minds to something without realizing they have done it. You can assume you would not enjoy learning something new because something similar did not interest you before. You might tell yourself that that new technology is too complicated, or that trying something different will take too much time, or that you already know enough about something and have decided it's not relevant. None of those thoughts feel unreasonable, which is exactly why they are so limiting. At the same time, they narrow what you are willing to explore and what you allow yourself to experience.

This matters even more now because the world around you is changing quickly. There are more ways to learn, more ways to contribute, and more ways to use what you already know than there have ever been before. There are also more reasons to tell yourself that something is not for you or not worth your attention. When your assumptions take over, you can miss opportunities without ever realizing they were even options in the first place, which makes it harder to adapt.

One of the most common assumptions I see right now is the belief that something will not impact you. You might look at artificial intelligence, new platforms, or new ways of doing things and assume you don't need to learn about them. You may tell yourself that younger people will understand them better, that technical people are better suited for learning those kinds of things, or that you are too far along in your current path in life to start learning something different. Those thoughts can feel so natural that you do not question them and begin to filter what you pay attention to and what you dismiss without thinking twice.

Another assumption is that you already know how something will end up. For example, instead of asking whether technology might help you, you decide it won't before even giving it a chance. Over time, that can make your world feel smaller, even when there are more possibilities available than ever before.

Your assumptions can also make you focus on the effort involved in adopting something new. You immediately think about how much time it might require, how steep the learning curve might be, and how frustrating it could feel in the beginning. Before you have even given something a chance, you have already decided it is more work than you want to deal with. You are not usually deciding whether to invest months or years, as most decisions are about trying something small. If you allow yourself to take that first step, it could change your perception of the experience by replacing uncertainty with something real.

Your experience plays a major role in what you will try based on what you've come to believe you can do. Maybe you tried something once and it did not go well, or you felt uncomfortable, or you did not see results as quickly as you expected. That experience could become your reference point for all future decisions, and you might assume that trying something will have the same outcome. What gets lost in that kind of thinking is how much has changed since you originally tried something the first time. You have more knowledge, more context, and often better tools than you did before, and the situation itself may be very different. When you treat every new situation as if it mirrors the past, you remove the possibility of a different result before you even begin.

Another common assumption is that you already understand something well enough to decide about whether it is worth exploring. You might read a short article, watch a brief video, or hear someone explain something and feel that you have the full picture. Based on that limited exposure, you decide whether it is useful or worth your time. Most things have far more depth than what you first notice, and that surface-level understanding rarely tells you how something could be useful to you in your life. When you base your decision on a first impression, you can easily overlook something that could have been valuable in ways you did not expect.

Assumptions also impact how you see yourself. One thing I have seen repeatedly is that people often decide once and then don't consider that decision again. You might decide you are not good at something, not interested in something, or that something is not relevant, and then move on. Many years later, you are still living with that same decision even though everything around you has changed.

You might not even think of it as a decision anymore, but as who you are. You may have decided at some point that you are not creative, not technical, or not someone who adapts easily to change. Those labels can become part of how you describe yourself, and over time they determine what you are willing to try and what you avoid altogether. However, those abilities are not fixed traits and develop through use, and the more you engage in creative thinking, problem solving, or learning new tools, the more comfortable you are doing those things. When you assume you do not have those abilities, you often avoid the very experiences that would help you build them in the first place.

There is another piece to this that is easy to miss. Assumptions do not feel like decisions because they feel like facts. Once you decide something is not for you, too difficult, or not worth your time, you stop looking for evidence that might prove you wrong. Assumptions are powerful because they remove options without you feeling like you made a choice.

The way to deal with this is not to force yourself into things you have no interest in, but to question why you think something is not for you. When you think something will take too much time, it helps to try a small part of it instead of the whole thing. When you believe you already understand something, it helps to ask what you might be missing and whether a little more exploration might change your perspective.

Those kinds of questions help you see that something different can happen when you look at what you tell yourself. Instead of deciding in advance, you can give yourself a chance to see what is there. Instead of assuming something is true, you question it. Instead of closing the door on an opportunity, you leave it open long enough to find out if it is worth walking through.

Over time, this changes how you interact with the world around you. It becomes easier to learn because you are more open to new ideas. It becomes easier to adapt because you are not locked into old conclusions that no longer serve you. It also becomes easier to find ways to contribute, because you are no longer limiting yourself based on what you assumed you could or could not do.

This matters because the next section of this book focuses on how you find meaning through exploration, connection, creation, and influence. If you never question your assumptions, you limit your options before you ever try anything. Think about people who back themselves into a corner. I have people ask me for work advice quite often, but once I start making suggestions, you can feel their walls go up and they often have similar responses: *I don't think I'd like that. That doesn't sound like something I could do. I wouldn't be good at that.* They are limiting their choices without even giving them a chance.

To keep options open, you must take action. It helps to recognize those negative voices and take opportunities to try new things, connect with people you might not normally connect with, and encourage yourself to open your mind to see how you can contribute to something. If assumptions are telling you those paths are not for you, too difficult, or not worth the effort, you may never take that first step, even when those paths are exactly what would bring more meaning into your life.

Working through your assumptions means giving yourself the chance to discover what might interest you before you decide what won't. You do not have to commit to anything long term. You are simply giving yourself enough room to find out what is true for you, which puts you in a much stronger position as the world continues to change.

CHAPTER 14

Technology

There has never been a time when technology has had a greater impact on how you live and work. It affects nearly everything you do and often makes life easier. It helps you move faster, access information instantly, and complete tasks that used to take hours in a fraction of the time. That can sound like progress, and in many ways it is. At the same time, it introduces a problem that is much harder to recognize because it does not feel like a problem when it is happening.

Most people assume they are in control of how they use technology. In many cases, they might be, but it can be harder to see how much you might overuse technology, as it can replace parts of your thinking without you realizing it. This is not obvious because it feels efficient. Technology feels helpful because it saves you time, but it can also change how you approach problems and how much you rely on your own thinking.

When thinking about over-reliance on technology, I am not referring to getting lost in scrolling and streaming. Instead, I am referring to letting it do your thinking for you. You might use it as a calculator, a life coach, a tutor, and before you know it, you stop questioning the why behind the output it gives you. It can free up your time, but it might be giving you inaccurate information or doing things for you that would otherwise make your life more rewarding.

When you rely on technology too much, it can limit your ability to think critically, evaluate what is true, and question what you are seeing. You spend more time observing and less time participating. Instead of working through ideas, you begin to accept what is given to you. That shift happens gradually, which is why it is easy to miss. It does not feel like you are losing anything, but your ability to think for yourself can weaken if you are not paying attention.

At the same time, some people underutilize technology to the point where they miss what it could help them do. They avoid it because it feels overwhelming or unfamiliar. They assume it is too complicated or not relevant to them. That decision may feel reasonable, yet it can prevent them from taking advantage of tools that could remove routine work and give them more time to focus on things that require real thinking.

You probably know people who refuse to do things on their computer because they fear they will break it, so they avoid learning things that could make their life more efficient. Their ability to use technology is usually not the issue as much as their willingness to engage with it.

When you decide something is too hard or not worth your time, you stop exploring it. That is what makes underutilization just as limiting as overreliance.

I found it interesting to see how people responded to the technology-related results they got when they took the CCI assessment. People who consider themselves early adopters of technology are often the most surprised by their results. They assume that because they use technology frequently, they are using it to their advantage. What they do not always see is how often they rely on it without questioning it or how quickly they accept answers without thinking through them. At the same time, those who avoid technology aren't surprised by their scores, but they often don't recognize how much that choice limits their ability to grow and adapt.

One way to measure your relationship with technology is how much you meaningfully learn from it. If it gives you shortcuts so you can spend time doing more valuable things, that is great. If you learned how it came up with the answers it did, that is better.

The problem I see most often is that people skip the steps that help them see how the technology they use produces its results. When that foundation is missing, everything remains surface-level. You may be able to get answers quickly, but you are not building the kind of depth that allows you to use those answers in meaningful ways. That is where overreliance on technology can become a problem.

If you handed Albert Einstein a calculator and never taught him the math behind it, you would not get the same outcome. He might become the greatest calculator operator in the world but never build the kind of thinking that led to his life-changing discoveries. When you rely on intelligent machines without understanding how they produce what they share with you, you limit how effectively you can use that output.

It can be challenging to find balance, and this is where most people struggle without realizing why. You might feel overwhelmed by technology while also feeling like it knows more than you do. There are times when technology can easily do the work for you and allow you to move quickly onto something more important, but your critical thinking needs to determine if that is the best solution.

There are also times when you need to slow down and work through something yourself, so you understand how it works and why it works that way. When everything is automated, you lose the depth of what you understand. It is just as important to recognize when to let technology do more for you, because when nothing is automated, you spend time on things that are not as important.

Having taught at universities for decades, I found it interesting to see how students learned and when they relied on technology for an easy answer versus when they took the time to think critically and compare sources to gain real understanding. Many of them liked to cite Wikipedia because it was easy, but it can be inaccurate, and the only way to know that is to look at the sources behind it. Those who really wanted to understand a subject did not simply cite Wikipedia; they dug deeper to find the true answer.

It's also easy to spend your time just being busy utilizing technology and not necessarily being productive. With so much information available online, it is easy to feel like you are accomplishing tasks when you are just consuming. When you use technology to create, test, or build something, your experience changes because you become more involved in what you are doing instead of just relying on whatever systems like AI tell you.

Many people might feel pressured to keep up with new technological tools, as something is always being introduced. In the business world, it seems like as soon as you learn one version of software, it is already time to learn something new. As a result, many people just wait because they figure there will be another new version coming, but they end up learning nothing. When you do engage with new technology, you quickly realize you can't learn everything, so the better approach is to focus on the few tools that help you work better and build from there.

People who stay current, even in small ways, and who question why it matters to their success tend to do far better than those who either avoid technology altogether or rely on it without thinking. You build confidence by trying something, understanding the why behind what it offers, and then using your creativity to build on that. The problem is that many people wait until they feel ready. It is more important to start where you are now and learn as you go. That is what keeps you engaged and helps you avoid the habit of letting technology do everything for you.

Over time, those small adjustments change how you interact with technology. Instead of something that fills your time, it becomes something that supports what you want to do and gives your life more meaning. That means you are no longer reacting to what appears in front of you but choosing how you engage with it and how you use it. If you let technology replace your thinking, it becomes harder to find where you fit and how you contribute. If you avoid it, you limit what you can do in a world where it plays a central role.

Technology is designed to keep your attention. It is built to pull you in, keep you there, and move you from one thing to another. When you recognize that, it becomes easier to step back and ask yourself if what you are doing is useful or if you are simply filling time.

Technology is a major part of your world, whether you like it or not. You need to decide how to use it to reach your goals. When you stay involved in the thinking process, you strengthen your ability to learn, adapt, and contribute, which keeps you from becoming passive in a world that is moving quickly.

CHAPTER 15

Environment

When you think about how your environment impacts your curiosity, it is not just your current workplace or family situation. It includes every interaction you have ever had and every message you have absorbed over time. Everyone in your life impacts your curiosity, including your parents, siblings, teachers, friends, coworkers, bosses, and even the constant stream of opinions you see on social media. Those voices all combine to influence how you think about what is interesting, what is worth your time, and what feels safe to explore.

You might not think too much about those interactions because they feel like such a normal part of your daily life. But they build patterns that have been reinforced for years. Those patterns feel so familiar, you don't bother to question them.

It begins in our childhoods. If you look back, you might remember a time when you were excited about something and someone dismissed it, or a moment when you asked a question and the response made you hesitate to ask another. A sibling may have laughed at you, a teacher may have told you not to talk so much, or a parent may have unintentionally discouraged an interest because they saw a different path for you. None of those moments needed to be dramatic to have an impact on you, but they influenced what you chose to pursue.

Everyone learns quickly how to adjust behavior, and that adjustment becomes part of how you operate. If your curiosity leads to having others encourage you, you continue. If it leads to being criticized or shut down, you back off. You do not consciously decide to become less curious. You simply notice what feels welcome and what does not, and then respond to those signals.

As you get older, that outside influence subtly continues and embeds itself in your routines. You start to notice what people around you value and what gets rewarded. Even among your group of friends, certain activities are favored more than others. At work, some behaviors like asking questions can create friction, and this negative feeling can be discouraging.

Social media adds another layer because you are constantly exposed to what other people tell you is important. There is no end to the constant barrage of opinions, and when you add algorithms that reinforce confirmation bias, social media platforms determine what you read and how you think. Even if you might feel a brief spark of interest in something, if it does not align with what you see others focusing on, you may not give it the time it deserves.

All of this creates patterns in your life, and those patterns turn into routines that guide your behavior in ways you don't even notice. You spend your day interacting with similar ideas, similar conversations, and similar expectations. Your routine makes you efficient, but it also narrows what you notice, which makes you operate within a smaller range of possibilities without realizing that your range has been impacted.

Your environment limits curiosity because it teaches you what feels acceptable, expected, and safe. If you grew up in an environment where technology was viewed as unnecessary or even threatening, you may still carry that belief even as intelligent systems have become the norm. If you have been in environments where following instructions mattered more than asking questions, it makes sense to hesitate when exploring or asking questions beyond what feels safe.

The problem is you are now living in a world where intelligent machines are becoming part of nearly every aspect of life, including the workplace and your home. When our environment changes, we must change to keep up with it. Intelligent systems can now generate ideas, analyze data, and perform tasks that once required years of training. Where does that leave us if we don't adapt? If your routines keep you anchored in old ways of doing things, this new world will be extremely challenging for many of you.

This is where adaptive curiosity can make an impact. Adaptive curiosity helps you remain open to recognizing the impact of that change and adjusting to it. It lets you look at everything that might initially feel unfamiliar and consider how you can use it to make your life more meaningful.

I often get asked by people taking the CCI whether they can do anything about what happened in their childhood. That is an important consideration because while you cannot go back and change the environment that shaped you, you can change how you respond to it now. When you start noticing how your routines influence your behavior, you can create the opportunity to make different choices. You can begin separating what you believe from what you were told to believe over time.

That awareness is practical because you might tend to avoid certain topics, tools, or conversations that could add depth to your life. When you explore the road that got you here, you may recognize that some of the routines you have developed leave little room for exploration. When you realize that you are relying on the same sources of information day after day, you can do something about that so that you can grow and avoid confirmation bias.

One way to begin shifting this is by looking at what you are consistently exposed to. If the same ideas and perspectives are part of your everyday, your thinking will not grow. Expanding that exposure might mean that you take some time to read something outside of your usual interests, listen to a different type of podcast, or spend time understanding how someone in another field approaches a problem. The goal is to widen your perspective just enough that you begin to see options you were not aware of before.

Paying attention to your routines also helps. Some people heavily rely on being so structured, they don't think they have time to incorporate more curiosity into their lives. Creating even a small amount of time to explore an idea or learn something unfamiliar can begin to change that. Those moments do not need to take up a lot of your time. What matters is that they happen consistently enough to shift your thinking.

The people you interact with also influence how you think. I'm not suggesting you change your friends or relationships, but you can change the kinds of conversations you have. You can also seek out mentorship from people who are different from you. If you are the smartest person you know, you need to expand your relationships. When you engage with people who approach problems differently or who are experimenting with new ideas, it introduces perspectives that can expand your own thinking. Those conversations often reveal possibilities that you would not have discovered on your own.

Over time, these adjustments you make can begin to change your relationship with your environment. You notice more, question more, and explore more. Your routines can begin to support your curiosity instead of limiting it, and that shift becomes increasingly important as the world around you continues to evolve.

This matters because the next section of this book focuses on how you find meaning through pathways that require engagement. That means you will need to try things, connect with different people, and use your ideas in ways that your past environment might have discouraged.

When you begin to adjust your old patterns, even in small ways, you create room for more possibilities. You start to recognize that you are not limited by what you have been told to think or exposed to in the past. You can explore new ideas, develop new skills, and contribute in ways that may not have been part of what you thought was possible for you.

Technology will continue to advance, and if your routines are built around old assumptions, it will be difficult to keep up with that change. It can feel very overwhelming to many of you right now. But when you evaluate your environment with adaptive curiosity, you give yourself the ability to consider adjusting, learning, and remaining engaged rather than feeling left behind.

PART IV

Developing Adaptive Curiosity

CHAPTER 16

Learning Again as an Adult

Many years ago, I had a conversation with a man named Brian Fabiano, who wrote the book *Neuromarketology*. We talked about the future of education, and I remember how we both believed that learning would become something people built for themselves instead of something handed to them in one place. We envisioned that you would not rely on one university or one program to give you everything. Instead, you would choose from different sources based on what you needed and what interested you at the time. Back then it sounded like a prediction, but today it is simply how many people learn.

If you think about learning something today, it probably feels different from how you learned when you were young. You don't intentionally follow a set path that was designed for you by someone else. You might look something up because you are curious about it, and before you know it, you're reading something else, or watching another video, or exploring content just to see what interests you. Sometimes you dig deeper into a topic and sometimes you don't, but the whole process feels more like following your interest than following a plan, and that's a very different way of learning than what you were used to growing up.

When you were younger, how you learned was designed by someone else. As you moved from one grade to the next, it felt like progress because you were given grades that told you how well you understood something, and you didn't have to figure out a path on your own. You just followed what was put in front of you, and that made it easier to feel like you were doing what you were supposed to be doing.

When progress is determined by someone else and that goes away, it can feel uncomfortable. You probably got used to thinking that getting through assignments and assessments meant you were growing. Once that structure disappeared, it became easy to feel a bit lost because you were used to following a system. That discomfort can be confusing, because even if your capability has not changed, you can feel like something important is missing.

I saw this coming when I was an MBA program chair more than a decade ago. Even then, it was clear that something was shifting in how people would need to learn. One of the biggest changes I wanted to make was to bring more behavioral development into graduate programs. I wanted students to spend more time on soft skills including emotional intelligence, critical thinking, and learning how to handle situations where there is no obvious answer. Those are the moments people face most often once they leave school, and they must rely on skills they have had the least practice developing.

At the time, that idea felt like it was pushing against the system. Graduate programs were built around expertise, content, and measurable outcomes. It made sense because that is how education had always been structured. Yet the more I worked with students, the more I saw that knowing information was only part of what they needed. Where they struggled most were the situations with no clear answer, no rubric, and no obvious path forward. Those were the moments where curiosity, adaptability, and confidence mattered far more than memorization.

I once interviewed John Couch, who had served as Apple Computer's first Vice President of Education. John told me that education has trained people to rely on memorization as a shortcut to success, rewarding students for repeating formulas rather than understanding how to think. He shared how he used to memorize everything in subjects like physics and chemistry, which worked until he faced a college exam question that required reasoning instead of recall, and he panicked. That experience exposed the flaw in the system: Students are conditioned to store and regurgitate information, but when faced with real problems that require thinking, visualization, and problem-solving, that approach breaks down. John and I agreed that students could benefit from developing their curiosity.

At around that same time, I also interviewed emotional intelligence author, Daniel Goleman, who told me that he believed curiosity would be one of the most important competencies of the future. Curiosity was not as popularly discussed then, and having someone like Daniel emphasize the importance of it was something I was thrilled to hear. Now you hear about curiosity everywhere, and that change reflects how much the expectations around learning and thinking have shifted.

Part of the reason this shift has happened is we have learned more about the value of curiosity and its impact on creativity. There was a popular study conducted by George Land who worked with NASA to study creativity in children. His results were startling because he found that when kids were very young, most of them demonstrated what he called genius-level creative thinking. As they moved through school, that number dropped dramatically. By adulthood, only a very small percentage still showed that same level of creative thinking.

Research shows that a similar thing happens with curiosity. Young children ask hundreds of questions each day, but then something happens when they become school-aged. Sir Ken Robinson addressed this issue in his popular TED talk. He said he believed education systems push people out of their natural creativity competencies. That is a strong statement, but when you think about how much emphasis is placed on getting the right answer, as John had mentioned, instead of exploring possibilities, it starts to make sense. When learning becomes tied to performance and evaluation, people approach it differently. They become more cautious, more aware of how they might be judged, and less willing to take the kinds of risks that lead to discovery.

You can probably see that difference in yourself. Think about how you approached learning when you were younger compared to how you approach it now. As a kid, you tried things without worrying too much about how good you were. You made mistakes, adjusted, and kept going until something clicked. You were not thinking about how it looked or how it compared to someone else. You were just doing what felt natural to you.

As you got older, that changed. Learning became tied to performance. You started to think about whether you should already have known something before you tried it. You became more aware of how things reflect on your abilities and how people might view you. That hesitation feels reasonable, but it can also slow you down in ways that are easy to miss.

In everyday situations, there are things you have thought about learning or ideas that have caught your attention, and you may have told yourself you would get to them when you had more time. Time passes, and you realize you stayed focused on what is already familiar because it is easier to continue doing what you already understand. When everything feels like an option, it can also be harder to decide where to start, and many people respond to that by not starting at all.

That pattern connects directly to the FATE factors you learned about in the last section of this book. There are moments when you hesitate because something feels unfamiliar. There are times when you decide something is not worth the effort before giving it a real chance. It becomes easy to rely on quick answers instead of working through something yourself, and your environment can either support what you are trying to do or pull you back into what is already comfortable.

Once you notice how the factors that inhibit curiosity create patterns, you begin to recognize small choices you make, like putting something off because it feels unfamiliar, brushing past an idea before giving it a real chance, or accepting an answer just to move on instead of really understanding it. Each of those decisions can feel like they aren't a big deal in the moment, yet over time they begin to influence how you approach learning without you even realizing it.

You may start to notice that the things you keep circling back to are not random. There are reasons a question sticks with you, or an idea keeps coming up. When you give these things a little more time instead of brushing them aside, and take small steps toward them without expecting to be perfect right away, that simple shift makes it easier to keep going.

As you do this more often, your confidence tends to build. You begin to trust yourself to figure things out as you go instead of waiting until everything feels clear ahead of time, and you get more comfortable being in the middle of learning. That is usually when you notice real progress, not just in what you know, but in how you approach it.

This matters even more now because intelligent systems can provide answers so quickly. Getting information is no longer the challenge you face. Deciding what to do with that information is where your real growth begins. You can look something up and move on, or you can stay with it long enough to make sense of it in your own way. That extra step is where what you learn begins to build your confidence, and it makes it easier to keep going instead of stopping once you have an answer.

What most people need at this point is not more information, but a way to decide what is worth learning and how to stay with the process of considering the value of that information long enough to make it meaningful. That is where many people get stuck, because they are still waiting for the kind of structure they had when they were younger. Since that structure is not coming back any time soon, you will need to create it in a different way for yourself.

You can start by noticing patterns in your own behavior. There are topics you come back to without anyone asking you to, problems that hold your attention longer than others, and ideas that stay on your mind even when you are not trying to think about them. Those patterns are easy to overlook, yet they often reflect what you are most likely to stay engaged with if you follow them a little further.

It can also help to ease up on the idea of how much you should be learning at once. Rather than thinking about mastering something, you can spend time understanding one part of it, try it out, and see how it fits. If it keeps your attention, you continue. If it doesn't, you move on without feeling like you failed, and that makes it easier to learn something new in the first place.

How you approach learning will become even more important as the world around you continues to change. Intelligent systems are already taking on tasks that once required significant time and effort. That will likely continue. What they do not replace is your ability to decide what matters to you and how you want to engage with it.

When you start to look at learning this way, it feels less like following a path and more like shaping one as you go. You are not waiting for someone to define what comes next. You notice what draws your interest, spend time with it, and stay with it long enough to see what you can build from it.

That may feel unfamiliar at first, especially if you have spent most of your life in structured environments. At the same time, it gives you a level of control that was not there before. You can shape your own direction in a way that fits how you think, what you value, and where you want to go.

When you begin to approach learning this way, it starts to feel more natural again. You are paying attention to what holds your attention and following it far enough to see where it leads. That is what allows you to keep moving forward, even when everything around you continues to change.

CHAPTER 17

Artificial Curiosity and Working with Intelligent Machines

You may have spent years believing that one of the safest places to be in your career was on the side of curiosity and creativity. You might have been told that if you could think, ask questions, and come up with new ideas, you would always have a place that machines could not reach. That belief has been repeated in classrooms, leadership books, and conference stages for years, and it has felt reassuring because it suggested there was a clear line between what people do and what technology can do.

That line is beginning to feel less certain, and if you pay attention to what is happening now, you are no longer just seeing systems handle repetitive tasks or follow strict instructions. They now generate options, test different approaches, and move toward something new without being told exactly how to get there. That change is subtle, but it changes how people interpret what these systems are capable of doing. It also creates a moment where you may find yourself wondering whether the qualities you believed made you valuable are still as protected as they once seemed.

To understand why this feels different, it helps to look at how researchers have begun exploring something called artificial curiosity. Several years ago, researchers at OpenAI and the University of California Berkeley designed an experiment to see what would happen if a system was rewarded for discovering something unexpected rather than completing a task. Instead of telling the system to win or reach a specific outcome, they rewarded it when its predictions about what would happen next were wrong. In other words, the system received a signal that encouraged it to move toward situations it did not fully understand.

As the system interacted with its environment, it began to behave in ways that looked surprisingly familiar. When it stayed in areas it had already experienced, its predictions improved and the reward decreased. When it moved into unfamiliar territory, its predictions were less accurate, which increased the reward. Over time, the system began to explore more broadly, not because it had been told to, but because it was driven to reduce uncertainty in what it encountered.

At a glance, that behavior can look a lot like curiosity, especially when you see the system testing, adjusting, and moving toward new experiences instead of repeating the same action. It is learning from what happens and using that information to guide what it does next, which can feel uncomfortably close to how people describe their own process of learning and exploration.

That is where confusion often begins, because the behavior may look similar, but the underlying experience is very different. The system is not wondering why something matters, choosing what is meaningful, or reflecting on how what it discovers connects to a broader purpose. It is responding to signals that reward novelty and prediction error. It is exploring patterns, not meaning.

The real difference appears when you compare how people experience curiosity with how a system processes information. Human curiosity is not only about encountering something new.

It involves interpretation, intention, and connection. When you explore an idea, you are not simply reacting to what is unfamiliar. You are deciding whether it is worth your attention. You are relating it to what you already know, what you care about, and what you want to contribute. Your curiosity is shaped by your experiences, your relationships, and your sense of purpose.

A system can move toward what it does not understand, but it does not decide why that matters or attach value to what it finds, and it does not experience satisfaction from helping someone else grow, creating something that reflects who it is, or influencing a situation meaningfully. Those elements are not part of the process it follows.

This becomes clear in how people use curiosity in real life. When you learn something new, it often leads you somewhere. You may apply that knowledge to solve a problem, help another person, or create something that did not exist before. The exploration is connected to an outcome that has meaning beyond the act of discovering information.

The system in the experiment was not doing that, because it was exploring to reduce uncertainty based on how it was rewarded, without choosing a direction based on values or purpose, and it simply followed the signal it was given.

This difference matters even more in your work, especially as systems begin to influence how problems are approached and solved across different roles. For years, people believed their advantage came from their ability to think through problems, generate ideas, and approach situations in creative ways. As systems begin to produce options and test possibilities at a much faster pace, the advantage begins to change, as it no longer comes from being the only source of ideas or exploration. It comes from how people interpret, guide, and apply what is generated.

Adaptive curiosity takes on a different role here, because your contribution is no longer centered on producing every answer yourself. Instead of relying on your ability to come up with every answer on your own, you begin to rely on your ability to ask better questions, recognize what matters, and connect ideas across different contexts. You move from being the sole source of output to becoming the person who shapes how that output is used.

You can see this play out across different roles. If you work in marketing, you may have spent years learning how to develop campaigns, write content, and analyze what resonates with an audience. Today, systems can generate multiple variations of messaging in seconds. That does not eliminate your role – it changes it. Your value comes from understanding which message aligns with the audience, how it fits into a broader strategy, and what direction will create the most meaningful impact.

If you teach, you may notice that information is now more accessible than ever. Students can find explanations, summaries, and examples quickly. Your role becomes less about delivering information and more about helping them interpret it, apply it, and connect it to their own experiences. You guide how they think rather than simply providing what they need to know.

If you lead a team, you may find that data and analysis are available at a level that once required significant time and effort. Your role shifts toward deciding which insights matter, how they should influence decisions, and how to align people around a shared direction. Rather than just processing information, you are shaping how it is used.

Across all these examples, the pattern is similar, because the system can explore options while you determine what those options mean, and that difference shapes how you contribute in a world where both are working side by side. Your adaptive curiosity allows you to stay engaged with what is changing, learn how to use new tools, and remain open to different ways of working while recognizing where your contribution fits within that environment.

As people begin to understand this change, their fear that they will be replaced by a system often gives way to a different realization. The question is no longer whether the system can do part of the work but how you position yourself in relation to what it can do.

That does not mean every role will remain the same, because some tasks will be handled differently and some responsibilities will change, while the need for interpretation, direction, and meaning remains consistent.

You can see this clearly when you think about situations where judgment matters. A system may generate several possible solutions to a problem, but it does not decide which one aligns with a specific set of values or long-term goals. It does not weigh how a decision will affect relationships, trust, or the experience of the people involved. Those considerations require a level of understanding that goes beyond pattern recognition.

People still have an advantage that is easy to overlook, especially when you consider how much of your work depends on context, relationships, and interpretation. You bring context to what you see. You understand nuance. You recognize how different factors interact in ways that are not always obvious. You also care about outcomes in a way that influences how you act. That combination influences how you use curiosity.

When you approach a situation, your curiosity is impacted by what you believe is important. You may explore an idea because it helps someone else, because it aligns with your goals, or because it contributes to something larger than yourself. That sense of direction guides where you focus your attention and how you use what you learn.

A system does not operate that way, because it does not bring context, intention, or a sense of purpose to what it is doing. It follows the structure it has been given, and even when that structure allows it to move toward novelty, it is still operating within a defined set of signals and responding to input rather than choosing meaning.

When you understand that difference, it becomes easier to see how you can work alongside these systems rather than feeling as though you are competing with them, and that changes how you approach your role. Your role becomes more about guiding the process than producing every element within it. You can use systems to expand what you are able to do while focusing your energy on the parts that require judgment, connection, and purpose.

This requires a change in how you think about your own value, especially if you have spent years defining that value based on specific tasks or outputs. If you define yourself only by the tasks you perform, any change to those tasks can feel threatening. If you define yourself by how you think, how you interpret, and how you contribute, your role becomes more flexible. You can move with the changes rather than resist them.

Adaptive curiosity supports that change by encouraging you to stay open to learning, experiment with new approaches, and continue developing your ability to connect ideas, while helping you see systems as tools that expand your capabilities rather than as replacements for what you do.

That perspective becomes especially important as these systems continue to improve, because they will expand what is possible while also changing how roles are defined. They will become faster at generating options and better at identifying patterns, and they will continue to influence how work is done across different fields; yet they do not replace the need for people to decide what matters and why.

When you think about your own work, consider where that distinction appears, because that awareness helps you see how your contribution can continue to evolve. Where are you generating output that could be supported by a system? Where are you making decisions that require understanding, context, or judgment? Where does your contribution involve helping someone else, creating something meaningful, or influencing an outcome in a way that reflects your perspective?

Those questions help you see how your role can evolve rather than disappear, and make it easier to stay engaged as changes continue to unfold. As you continue through this book, you will explore different ways people find meaning through exploration, connection, creation, and influence. Each of those areas reflects something that extends beyond pattern recognition. They involve how you engage with the world, how you interact with others, and how you contribute to something that matters.

Artificial curiosity may allow systems to explore in ways that appear similar on the surface, but it does not replace the human experience of meaning that gives that exploration direction. When you recognize that difference, you can see how you fit into a world where intelligent machines play a larger role and focus on how you use what they produce to reflect your understanding, your relationships, and your sense of purpose.

That is where your role continues to evolve, as you focus more on how you guide, interpret, and apply what these systems produce, and it is where your ability to remain curious, adaptable, and engaged becomes one of the most important factors in how you move forward in a world where intelligent systems continue to expand what is possible.

CHAPTER 18

The Real Reason You Don't Start Anything New

Something can feel like a good idea right up until the moment it becomes real. That is usually when you start thinking about what it will actually require and whether you want to take that on.

One of the biggest honors I have received caused me to question whether I wanted to accept it. I remember exactly how it felt when I got the email that I had been selected to receive the Fulbright Specialist award. That meant a lot to me to be recognized like that, and it sounded like an exciting opportunity. But the moment it became a real possibility, everything about it shifted in my mind. Taking on that responsibility meant leaving for two weeks and traveling to a country I had never been to. I travel quite often for work by myself, but usually for just a few days at a time, and I could feel my hesitation almost immediately.

Like many people might do, I put together a case for why I shouldn't go in my mind. I had responsibilities and a schedule that would mean two weeks of unpaid work, along with a number of other reasons to justify not going. No one would have questioned it if I turned it down, and that made it even easier to consider saying no. I started thinking less about the amazing people I would meet and the impact I could hopefully make, and more about the downsides. I started to think about the potential grueling schedules, and the inconvenience of not being at home to do the rest of my work like grading and keeping up with my other job responsibilities from a hotel room. I knew there would be several days I would have to get up at 3 a.m. just to keep up with it all.

I chose to go anyway, and I can still remember what it felt like to be there by myself, navigating something completely outside of what felt normal. It was uncomfortable at first, and there were moments where I questioned whether I had made the right decision, mostly when I was typing away at 3a.m. Then, something started to change as I began working with people I would never have met otherwise and connecting with organizations from completely different parts of the world. The conversations were different, the problems were different, and the way I saw my own work started to shift. That experience became one of the most meaningful things I have done, and it only happened because I allowed myself to get past that first reaction to say no and stepped back to think about what I would be missing if I turned it down.

What stands out to me now is how I could have said no without ever realizing what I was walking away from. You might say no more than you realize. Something might catch your attention, you can see yourself doing it, and as soon as it becomes something that could be real, you start explaining to yourself why it does not make sense right now. The explanation sounds reasonable, so you accept it and move on.

When you look at how often this happens, a pattern becomes hard to ignore. You revisit the same ideas more than once, you think about them in different situations, and you talk about them as if you might do them someday. You stay close enough to feel interested, yet you never get close enough to experience anything real. Over time, you build a list of things you almost did, and that list starts to define how far you push the edges of your life.

This pattern starts earlier than you think, and it happens faster than you realize. The moment something new appears, your mind begins evaluating it based on what you already know and how you expect yourself to perform. You compare it to your current level of ability, how long it might take to feel comfortable, and whether you will look competent while you are learning. That process happens automatically, and it decides what you feel next. This keeps happening because you are protecting the version of yourself that already feels capable, and that protection limits what you allow yourself to try.

You can probably think of several things right now that you said you wanted to try and never started. If you go back to those moments, you can find the point where something shifted. You saw someone else do it and decided you should already be at that level. You remembered a past experience and decided you did not want to feel that way again. You made a quick call about what it would take, and you treated it as fact. You moved on without ever testing whether any of it was true.

We don't just do this when deciding what to do about big opportunities. There is a smaller version of this you might recognize. You open a book, read the first few pages, and close it because it feels like more than you want to deal with right now. You start a conversation with someone new and pull back when it feels uncertain. You consider reaching out, asking a question, or offering an idea, and you decide to wait for a better moment. Those moments feel small, yet they follow the same pattern as the bigger decisions. You step back before anything has a chance to develop, and you repeat that pattern often enough that it becomes your default.

As you gain more experience, this becomes stronger in ways that are easy to miss. You get used to being capable, used to knowing what you are doing, and used to being someone others rely on. That becomes part of how you define yourself, even if you never say it directly. Then something new comes along and you find yourself in a position where you do not have answers yet. That gap feels uncomfortable because it does not match the identity you have built. You measure yourself against your most experienced self, and that comparison stops you before you even begin.

You can see this clearly when someone who has been successful for years tries something new. They go from being confident and respected to asking basic questions again, and that shift feels larger than it actually is. They are learning the same way they always have, yet it feels different because they are aware of the contrast. You might recognize that feeling, where something simple like asking for help feels more uncomfortable than it should. What you are doing is protecting your identity, but that is what keeps you from expanding it.

You move through the early stage of learning with a sense of urgency that works against you. You expect to feel capable quickly, and when that does not happen, you start questioning whether the effort makes sense. That early discomfort becomes something you interpret as a signal instead of recognizing that this is where learning starts. You begin judging the entire experience based on how it feels in the beginning. What you are doing is deciding too early, before anything meaningful has had time to develop.

The people you spend time around influence this more than you probably realize. When you are surrounded by people who stay within what they already know, that becomes the standard. You rarely see anyone trying something new, struggling with it, and continuing long enough to improve. That absence reinforces hesitation because it normalizes staying where you are. When you are around people who regularly try new things, the experience shifts because you see a different pattern in action. You begin to feel more open to doing the same.

When you recognize this pattern in real time, you can interrupt it. The moment you feel yourself pulling back, consider the opportunity long enough to experience something real instead of relying on your first reaction. Think about just a small part of it, ask a specific question, or spend time with it without expecting immediate results. That replaces your assumptions with experience. You begin forming your opinion based on what it actually is instead of what you imagine it is.

This becomes more important as change continues to accelerate. When you avoid starting, you reduce the range of what you are able to do over time. When you begin, even when it feels unfamiliar, you expand that range and create options that would not have existed otherwise. The difference between those paths often comes down to how you respond in that first moment.

When you look back at things you have learned before, you can see this pattern clearly. There was a point where you did not know what you were doing, where it felt uncomfortable, and where it would have been easy to stop. You stayed with it long enough for it to make sense, which built confidence over time. That early stage has always been part of the process. When you allow yourself to move through it again, you give yourself the chance to grow in new directions.

As you continue, a different kind of confidence begins to develop. It comes from knowing you can try something unfamiliar and stay with it long enough to figure it out. That confidence is not tied to any one skill, and it does not depend on already being good at something. It grows from experience and from the willingness to begin before everything feels certain. You stop treating your first reaction as a final answer and start using it as a starting point.

This connects directly to how you experience meaning. The experiences you allow yourself to have are the ones that reveal what actually engages you. You begin to notice where your energy increases, where your attention holds, and where your effort feels worthwhile. Those patterns become clear when you have enough real experience to compare.

As you move forward, you start to see patterns in what draws you in and what you return to. At times, it comes from exploring an idea long enough to understand something new, and at other times, it grows out of a conversation. There are moments when building or creating something holds your attention, and others where guiding people or shaping outcomes feels significant. You only see these patterns after you have stayed in enough situations to recognize them. When you step back too early, you never collect enough experience to see what actually matters to you.

The shift begins when you change the question you ask yourself. Instead of asking whether you will be good at something, you ask whether you are willing to stay with it long enough to learn from it. That question changes your approach because it removes the pressure to perform right away. You allow the experience to unfold and give yourself time to understand it. You begin making decisions based on what you experience instead of what you predict.

When you do that, your direction becomes clearer. You see where your interest deepens and where it fades. You understand what holds your attention when it becomes challenging and what you are willing to continue even when it takes effort. That clarity helps you move toward the experiences that actually matter to you.

You stop too early more often than you realize, and that choice shapes what you never end up experiencing. When you give something a little more time, you start to see what is actually there instead of what you assumed would be there. Over time, that changes how you make decisions. You rely less on your first reaction and more on what you have actually tried and seen for yourself. That shift is what opens up new directions, because you are no longer deciding based on what you think might happen. You are deciding based on what you now know from real experience.

CHAPTER 19

Overcoming Avoidance

My family has never been a big adopter of technology, and I have always found it interesting that my 93-year-old mother probably embraces it more than the rest of them. When I asked my cousin for his email, he said to me, "We don't own a computer box." He was not trying to be pretentious, funny, or even make a point. He simply had never used a computer, and because his life had been centered around sports instead of business, it never felt useful enough to learn.

My sister is also not a fan of computers, even though she used them for work because she had to. When she applied for a new job and wanted help preparing for her interview, I did not have much time to walk through it with her, so I suggested she use AI to get some practice questions. She was not excited about the idea but she tried it, and she was surprised not that it worked, but how quickly it worked. In a short amount of time, she felt more prepared than she expected, and her entire view of using it changed because she could finally see where it fit into something that mattered to her.

It is easy to say we do not like something when we do not see how it fits into our lives. If something does not feel relevant, it is easy to ignore, dismiss, or push it aside without much thought. In the past, it was far easier to put off embracing technology, because it wasn't such a big part of our lives. It was also far more challenging to learn. Today, technology itself can help you learn how to use it, but that requires you to explore how to let it help you.

That begins with building your adaptive curiosity. When I train people to overcome the factors that limit their curiosity, what helps most is recognizing that you can read about curiosity, talk about it, and even agree with everything you have learned so far, but nothing changes until you actually do something.

This usually starts with something simple, even if it does not feel that way at first. It comes from looking at the things you could have done but avoided, the moments you let pass without much thought. Maybe it was a tool that could have made your life easier, or a conversation you avoided that might have cleared something up. Most people do not spend much time thinking about these moments, but they add up and influence the direction your life takes more than you might expect.

It is very easy to come up with good reasons for not taking action, and most of them sound completely reasonable in the moment. You might tell yourself you need more time or more clarity before you begin, or you might spend time reading about something that could help and convince yourself that counts as progress. That part feels productive, and in some ways, it is, but it also keeps you in a place where nothing is really required of you. At some point, if you want something to actually change, you have to move past thinking about it and engage with it in a real way.

One of the biggest issues I see is how much time people spend observing instead of participating. It is easy to read about what others are doing, listen to ideas that make sense, and watch examples that feel motivating for a short time. That can feel like progress, but there is no risk in observing, which is why it is so comfortable, but that eventually leads to the feeling that something is missing.

In my training sessions, I have people look directly at what is keeping them stuck, which is where things begin to change.

We focus on what keeps them in the same patterns and identify one small step that would move them forward.

Those steps are usually much smaller than people expect, which is why they are often overlooked. A step might be trying something you have been putting off or finally using a tool you have avoided. Sometimes it means following an idea to see where it leads instead of continuing to analyze it, or reaching out to someone instead of waiting until you feel completely prepared. That is when things start to change, because you move from thinking about something to actually experiencing it.

As you begin to do that more consistently, adaptive curiosity starts to build in a way that feels real. You begin to see that even though technology may close some doors, it opens many more, and while some of those opportunities are difficult to see at first because things are changing so quickly, they are there. When you begin to engage instead of observe, you start to notice them in ways you would not have before.

At some point, you start to see the thing you are trying to achieve differently. Opportunities are not going to present themselves in a way that makes the next step obvious or comfortable. You have to decide to engage with what is already in front of you and see where it leads, even if you are not sure what will come from it.

You can see that in my sister's experience. She already had access to the technology. Nothing new was introduced to her, and nothing about the situation changed except how she saw it once she experienced it for herself. Once it mattered enough, something she had avoided became useful. As someone who loves to write, that one step opened up possibilities for ways she could use AI that she had not considered before.

If you have been hesitant to try something, whether it is technology or something else that could give your life more meaning, this is where you start to notice where you have been holding back. When you recognize that, you can start taking steps to create a future you might not have ever considered.

The question then becomes how you determine what matters most. In my work, I found that there are four ways people most often experience meaning, which include exploration, connection, creation, and influence. As you read about them, you will likely recognize which of those provide you with the most meaning in your life.

You are not going to find meaning by just thinking about those paths, because thinking will only keep you in the same place. You will only discover meaning by trying things, paying attention to how you respond, and adjusting based on what you learn. The moment you move toward meaning is when you stop explaining your hesitation and start trying something small, even if you are not sure how it will turn out, because that is what takes you from being an observer to becoming a participant in your own life.

Everything you have read so far has been leading to this point. If you feel stuck, it is because you are at the point where it becomes your decision to begin, and once you make that decision, you stop waiting for direction and start creating a life that feels more meaningful.

PART V

The Four Paths of Meaning

CHAPTER 20

Four Paths: The Meaning Alignment Profile (MAP)

Many of you probably watch TV, read articles, or see things on social media that predict the end of work as we know it. That can be very frightening. You might hear different timelines and conflicting opinions about when or if this will happen, but if technology significantly changes the workplace, and even potentially replaces human workers, how are we going to know what to do with ourselves? What will our days look like when the structure we have always known is no longer there?

I have always loved technology. If there is something new on the market, I want to try it. I look forward to seeing what cool new thing will come out to make life more interesting and potentially easier. Until recently, I had never really thought that technology could move so quickly and potentially replace all jobs. Even in *Star Trek*, people still went to work. They might have worked at Starfleet Academy teaching young cadets, but they had a job. Even Gene Roddenberry, who covered a lot of ground in his vision, never really addressed the possibility of most, if not all, jobs being replaced in the future.

If you are like me, you probably wonder what life would actually feel like on a normal day if that happened. If you wake up and there is nothing you have to do, how do you decide what you should do, and how do you make sure that what you choose actually feels meaningful instead of just filling time?

It's hard not to wonder what will happen, because there really is no road map for this. We have never had a moment quite like this where so much of what impacts your day could change so quickly. People have always had to adjust to new technologies, but this feels different because it is not just changing how we work. It is changing how we might spend most of our time.

When I thought about how to help people in this new reality, I wasn't trying to build a model or come up with a theory. I wanted something more practical than that. I wanted to share helpful advice, based on what I know about adapting using curiosity, so that if things do dramatically change, you will know how to find meaning in your life.

Many people have written about meaning and purpose, and I touch on that here, but I didn't want this to be a book analyzing theories of meaning. There are also a lot of books about curiosity, but most of them focus on what curiosity is and why it matters. My work has always been a little different. I have been more interested in what gets in the way of curiosity, how to overcome those issues, and how to build a culture that embraces it. This book takes on something else, too. It answers how to use curiosity to deal with change when the entire world might be something you don't recognize soon due to intelligent machines. If that happens, adaptive curiosity will become something you rely on to figure out what comes next.

The way I approached it was the same way I have approached other questions in my research. I asked people about their daily experiences to determine what gave them a sense of meaning. As I looked at those responses, I started to see patterns in how people described what made their days feel meaningful. If you want to see how you might respond, I included a set of questions in the appendix based on this research. You don't need to go through them now, but they can help you recognize yourself more clearly as you read through the next chapters.

That is what led me to the four paths that lead to meaning. I'll walk you through them in the next chapters in more detail, but it helps to have a simple sense of what each of these looks like and why they matter.

The first path is exploration. Exploration is what you feel when you are learning, asking questions, or trying to understand something more clearly. It helps to look at what others have found. Viktor Frankl, drawing from his time in Nazi concentration camps, observed that even in the darkest conditions, people who focused on something beyond themselves, something they were trying to understand, create, or move toward, were more likely to maintain a sense of purpose.

While this is hardly Nazi Germany, we are in a frightening time for many people, and there is still something important we can take from Frankl's work. What he showed is that focusing on something beyond yourself can create a sense of meaning even when things feel uncertain. Exploration does that in a very practical way. When you are learning, asking questions, or trying to understand something, you are not just passing time. You are moving toward something, and that sense of direction is a big part of what makes your time feel meaningful.

The second pathway is connection. Connection is found through your relationships and how you interact with other people. I interviewed Dr. Martin Seligman, who spent years studying well-being. He shared that relationships are one of the biggest contributors to a meaningful life, and what stood out to me was how much of that comes down to how we engage with others. He talked about how curious people ask better questions and create space for people to contribute, and that is where connection really starts to matter.

If you think about your own life, the moments that tend to impact you the most usually involve other people in some way. When you feel like you helped someone, supported someone, or even just had a conversation where you felt understood, that matters more than you expect. Meaning stems from moments where your time connects to someone else in a real way.

The third pathway is creation. Creation is what you experience when you build something, solve something, or complete something. Teresa Amabile, who studied motivation and performance, found that one of the strongest drivers of engagement is making progress on something that matters.

That is a simple but powerful idea. When you can see that something moved forward because of what you did, it changes how you experience your time. It does not have to be something big. Even small progress can shift your entire day, because you are not just busy. You can point to something and say it improved because of what you did, and that creates a sense that your time doing it counted.

The fourth pathway is influence. Influence is what you feel when you are involved with other people and you contribute to something bigger than you. It is interesting to look at what has been written about this as well. In addition to what you learned about Albert Bandura's work earlier, he also studied how people learn and influence each other. He found that people feel a stronger sense of purpose when they see that their actions have an impact.

Influence, in the way it is described here, is about being part of a team, a group, or even leading others in a positive way. When you can see that something has changed because you were part of it, it shifts how you experience what you are doing.

What makes this even more interesting is how these areas work together. Just like with the factors of FATE, these four pathways can also intersect. For example, you might learn something as a form of exploration and use it to help someone else as a form of connection. Or you might build something as a form of creation that impacts others as a form of influence. When these areas combine, the experience tends to feel stronger.

Research in positive psychology shows that meaning becomes stronger when purpose, relationships, accomplishment, and engagement come together. The more these elements combine, the more likely you are to feel a lasting sense of meaning. That helps explain why certain days stand out more than others, even when the amount of time you spent working was the same.

These are not labels you have to fit into. You are not one or the other. Everyone is a combination of all four, and you will probably recognize that pretty quickly as you read through them. You will likely have a sense of which of the four pathways fit you best, or even the top two. Recognizing that you are more drawn to those areas will help you understand what kinds of things bring you meaning.

When I looked through the responses from my research, one thing that stood out was how often meaning was tied to other people. People talked about feeling good when they helped someone succeed, and the satisfaction that comes with finishing something, building something, or contributing to a clear outcome.

Another thing that stood out was how different groups aligned. Women, on average, tended to lean slightly more toward connection, especially in areas involving relationships and support. Men showed a slightly stronger pull toward creation and influence, particularly when it came to building and driving outcomes. Those differences were not extreme, and they do not define any individual, but they were consistent enough to be worth noting.

What mattered most is that everyone showed meaningful engagement across all four areas. This led me to believe that you are not limited to one way of finding meaning, even if you naturally lean more toward one or two.

Something else I noticed is that meaning feels stronger when more than one of these areas is active at the same time. When you learn something and use it to help someone, or build something that affects a group, or contribute to something that grows out of curiosity, the experience tends to feel more complete. That overlap is often what separates an ordinary day from one that really stands out.

For a long time, work has made this easier without you having to think about it. Work gives you problems to solve, people to interact with, things to complete, and opportunities to contribute. It creates a rhythm that supports those experiences. However, if our world changes as dramatically as many predict, that rhythm may not guide you anymore.

It will be up to you to determine what your day entails, and that is where things can start to feel off for you. You might stay busy all day and still feel like nothing you did was worthwhile. That tends to happen when you do not feel engaged. If you notice that, you can change how you spend your time. You can go from simply filling your day to paying attention to the kinds of things that give you meaning. My hope is that this book will help you do that, so instead of wondering what to do with your time, you will have a clearer sense of where to start.

In the next four chapters, you will explore each of these pathways one at a time so that you can recognize what they look like in your own day and start using them to create a life that feels rewarding.

CHAPTER 21

Exploration

Imagine waking up one morning with no alarm, opening your eyes, and realizing there is nothing you have to do. There are no meetings waiting for you, no messages to respond to, and nothing from yesterday carrying over into today. You have a full day ahead that is completely open, which at first feels like freedom, so you might stay in bed a little longer and eventually get up and make coffee. You go through your morning randomly choosing things to occupy your time, but nothing feels all that important. As time passes, you experience a familiar feeling.

It is the same feeling you had as a kid on the first day of summer, part excitement and part uncertainty, because your routine is about to change and you do not yet know what will replace it. Nothing is really wrong, but the lack of direction makes you uneasy. That is when you start asking yourself, what am I going to do today?

If intelligent machines take over much of what people used to do, this could be a preview of what is to come. When the structure that once organized your days is gone, what do you do next? That question becomes more personal when your sense of meaning has been tied to discovery, because the way you experienced your day begins to change.

So many people think they want free time until they have it. What they really want is more control over how they spend their time. The problem is that once you have that control, it becomes your responsibility to provide the direction. When everything is an option, it can feel overwhelming, and people often end up circling through activities that never quite feel meaningful.

When intelligent machines begin doing much of what used to fill your day, that shift becomes more noticeable. Some of you will find that your roles change significantly, and others may find that you are no longer working in the same way at all. If your sense of meaning has been tied to discovery, that change can feel especially unsettling, because you may wonder what happens when systems do much of the discovering and you are left reviewing the results.

If you are not working, whether by choice or circumstance, you are now responsible for planning your entire day, and that can feel exhausting if you are used to having structure provided for you. At first you might describe that restless, sometimes empty feeling as boredom, but it is more tied to a lack of direction that leaves you with more time than you know how to fill.

As intelligent machines take over more things you used to do, you might need to make fewer decisions and exert less effort to get through your day. That creates space, and that space can feel either freeing or uncomfortable depending on how it is used. If nothing is pushing you, something has to pull you. Without that pull, time begins to feel empty even when it is full of activity.

You can already see this difference in how people respond to the same situation. Some people fill that space with distraction. They scroll, watch, react, and move from one thing to the next without much thought about where their time is going. At the end of the day, they may have been busy, but the experience becomes forgettable even though it was full.

Someone who is energized by exploration would likely respond differently. Instead of trying to fill time, they might begin by following something that catches their attention. It might start as a simple question, something that does not quite make sense or something they want to understand more clearly. They spend more time on it than most people would, look into it, and think about it more deeply. When they do that, they have unintentionally created a process that determines how they spend their time.

The difference between these two experiences is not intelligence, access, or opportunity. It is whether someone allows their attention to be directed for them or whether they take responsibility for directing it themselves. That distinction becomes more important when nothing external is organizing your time for you.

If you tend to lean toward exploration, you already know what this feels like. You are not satisfied with surface-level answers for very long, and distraction does not hold your attention because it does not lead anywhere. You want to understand how things work, why they work, and how they connect to something else you have seen before.

Exploration becomes the way you create direction when nothing else is providing it. It gives your day a sense of movement without requiring anyone else to define what that movement should be.

For many people, they seem content to move on even if they can't resolve the answer to a question. But, if you are energized by exploration, that is hard for you to do. Something that feels incomplete is hard to ignore, so instead of letting it go, you keep working through it, read more, think more, and begin to see it from different angles.

It might not seem like you have created a process because you are not checking something off a list or completing a task that someone assigned to you. And from the outside, it might look like you are simply spending time thinking or reading, yet from your perspective something is changing because you are beginning to understand something that was not clear before.

This is when you recognize that something you explored has held your attention longer than most things do. It becomes part of what you want to include in your day. That moment stands out because it shows that your time is no longer being filled at random. It is shaped by something that is pulling you forward.

You may also notice that when something truly captures your attention, it changes how you experience the rest of your day. A conversation you have later on might remind you of it, or something you read might suddenly connect back to it in a way that feels unexpected. That carryover matters because it shows that your time is not isolated into separate activities, and instead it begins to link together into something that feels continuous.

You have probably noticed that some days feel long even when you are busy, while other days seem to disappear even when you are focused on one thing. The difference usually has less to do with how much you accomplished and more to do with how connected you felt to what you were doing. When something holds your attention, you do not have to push yourself to keep exploring it. You continue because you want to, and that changes how you spend your time and that feeling you thought was boredom is replaced by the desire to learn more.

When you begin to structure your time around what holds your attention in that way, your days start to feel different. Instead of moving from one thing to the next, you find yourself returning to something that you can continue to develop. One idea leads to another, and something you read changes how you see something else.

Those moments begin to add up, and they create a sense that your time is building toward something. You start to recognize patterns, notice when something does not quite add up, and become more comfortable continuing to work through something before it is fully clear. That experience begins to shape how you approach problems, decisions, and even everyday conversations.

For those of you who embrace exploration, you are less likely to find satisfaction in distraction because that simply resets your attention. Exploration carries it forward. When your day is built around distraction, each activity stands alone and then disappears. When your day includes exploration, something from earlier continues into what you do next. That continuity is what gives your time meaning.

There is also a level of independence that develops along the way. When you rely on exploration, you are not waiting for someone else to tell you what to focus on next. If something matters to you, you follow it far enough to begin understanding it. That does not mean you ignore other people's input, but your sense of progress is not dependent on it.

You have likely experienced this when something stayed on your mind long after you tried to move on. It might have been a question that did not have an easy answer, a problem that did not resolve cleanly, or an idea that held your attention. That persistence is often a signal that there is something there worth understanding.

When that part of your experience is missing, time can start to feel repetitive in a way that is difficult to explain. You may still complete everything expected of you and remain busy throughout the day. But there is no sense that your understanding is changing or that your time is building toward something. Without that, even a full day can feel disconnected.

When exploration becomes part of your day, even small moments begin to feel meaningful. One question leads to another, a piece of information changes how you see something, and an idea opens up a direction you had not considered before. Those moments may not stand out to anyone else, but they stand out to you because they show movement.

They show that your time is going somewhere.

That sense of movement often becomes easier to recognize after you have experienced it a few times. You start to notice the difference between information that doesn't grab your attention and something that holds long enough to change how you think. When that difference becomes clear, it becomes easier to choose where to spend your time without needing someone else to guide you.

Exploration becomes more important in a world shaped by intelligent machines. As systems take over more routine tasks, you may find that less is required of you in the traditional sense. That can feel like a loss at first because so much of your identity may have been tied to what you were expected to do; yet it also creates an opening where you have to decide what is worth pursuing.

When systems can provide answers instantly, the temptation is to stop asking better questions. It is easy to accept what is given and move on. Over time, technology can remove the need for you to spend enough time with something to understand it, and that is where your ability to explore can be impacted.

If that happens, your time can feel efficient but empty. Things get done, yet nothing can feel as satisfying. That is why choosing what to explore becomes more important as machines become more capable. It is one of the few places where you still decide what is worth your attention.

Some people will try to fill that space as quickly as possible, looking for ways to stay occupied without thinking too much about what they are doing. Others will hesitate because they are not used to making those choices for themselves. Both responses are understandable because for most of your life direction was provided for you.

Exploration offers a different way forward because it replaces the need for external direction with something internal. Instead of asking what should I do today, you begin recognizing you should ask what you want to understand next.

When you begin following that, your time starts to organize itself in a different way. Instead of filling hours or reacting to whatever appears in front of you, you are continuing something that carries from one day to the next, even if that is simply a question you have not fully answered yet.

One way to recognize that your exploration is working is by noticing what continues to hold your attention later. You may find yourself returning to the same idea without effort, or noticing that something you learned changes how you interpret something else. That connection gives your time a sense of continuity.

Another sign is that your attention begins to settle instead of scatter. You may still explore broadly, yet you come back to certain areas more often than others. That pattern creates a sense of direction without requiring a formal plan.

If you are not sure where to begin, it helps to start smaller than you think you should. Think back to what you learned from Albert Bandura's work. Confidence develops through small steps, and the same idea applies here. You choose something that holds your attention and spend a little more time on it than you normally would.

At first, that may feel unfamiliar because you are used to having direction provided for you. Over time, that discomfort begins to fade, and your days begin to take on a different rhythm. They may not look as structured as they once did, but they feel more engaging because your attention has direction.

You are no longer trying to fill time because you are following something that continues. One question leads to another, and something that held your attention yesterday carries into what you do next. You return to it without forcing yourself to, and each time you do, your understanding deepens in a way that makes your time feel connected.

That is when you begin to recognize the difference. Your day is no longer a series of separate activities. It begins to feel like something that builds, even when there is no external structure guiding it. What you choose to explore becomes what shapes your time.

And once that starts to happen, the question that felt so open at the beginning of this chapter becomes easier to answer, because instead of asking what you should do, you are already following what you want to understand next.

CHAPTER 22

Connection

Imagine a day where nearly every hour is filled with some form of conversation. As soon as you wake up, you check your phone and respond to a few messages before you even have breakfast. Before long, you are moving from one conversation to another by responding to texts and emails, sitting through meetings that require your input, and spending much of your time talking, listening, or reacting to what people need. By the end of the day, you have spoken to more people than you can even count.

From the outside, it looks like a full day. You were responsive, involved, and present in everything that required your attention. If someone asked how your day went, you could point to how much you handled and how many people you interacted with. It would be easy to describe it as productive.

Yet when you slow down and think back on it, most of those interactions blend together. You remember pieces of conversations, but very few of them stand out. Then one comes back more clearly than the rest.

You remember how closely you were paying attention without trying. Something about that moment felt different. It may not have lasted very long, and nothing about it looked unusual from the outside, yet it was more meaningful.

If that experience feels familiar, it points to something important about how you experience meaning. For you, meaning often develops through moments of real connection, especially when something becomes clearer for the other person in a way you can feel.

You can have dozens of conversations in a day and forget most of them. They serve a purpose, they move things forward, and then they end. But every so often, there is a moment where something changes. The other person sees something differently, questions something they assumed was true, or softens the way they see themselves. You may not have planned for it, and you may not be able to explain exactly what you did, yet you know it happened.

That is the moment that stands out.

It might simply have been a short conversation where you didn't intend to give advice or come up with all the right words. But something changed for the other person, maybe just slightly, but since you were part of that moment, that had an impact on you.

Once you begin to notice that, it becomes easier to understand why some interactions feel meaningful and others do not. You can spend an entire day communicating without feeling any sense of depth, or you can have one conversation that changes how the day feels when you look back on it.

It shows you that meaning is not coming from the number of conversations you have. It comes from the moments where something real happens between you and someone else. Connection is strengthened when something you said or did created an impact.

When you are part of a meaningful conversation, you are paying attention in a different way. You listen more closely without forcing yourself to do it. You pick up on what is being said and what is not being said. You notice hesitation, tone shifts, and small changes that others may overlook. You respond in a way that fits what the other person actually needs in that moment, even if you cannot fully explain how you knew.

Those moments do not always stand out right away. Even if you move on with your day, later, you may find yourself replaying parts of the conversation and noticing what changed for the other person or how they responded. That is often when you recognize that the interaction had more of an impact than it seemed at the time.

Over time, those experiences begin to determine how you see yourself. You notice that people respond differently to you. They open up more easily, they return to you when something is important to them, and they trust you with things they may not share with others. That pattern builds gradually until it becomes clear that connection is one of the ways you create meaning.

You also notice when that part of your experience is missing. You can spend an entire day talking to people, responding to messages, and attending meetings, yet something feels off. The conversations happen, but nothing changes. Your attention moves on quickly, and nothing carries beyond the moment itself. Without that sense of impact, even a full day can feel disconnected.

That difference becomes easier to understand when you look at how your attention gets impacted. In routine interactions, your attention resets from one conversation to the next. Each exchange stands on its own and then fades. In meaningful interactions, something continues in your thinking, influencing what you notice afterward and how you interpret other situations. That continuation is what makes connection meaningful for you.

When an interaction has that kind of impact, it does not end when the conversation does. It influences what you think about later, how you interpret other interactions, and how you understand the person you spoke with. A single moment becomes part of a larger experience instead of something isolated.

When that does not happen, interactions can feel interchangeable. You respond, move on, and repeat the process without anything building from one moment to the next. Time passes, yet it does not feel connected to anything that continues.

As intelligent machines take on more of the communication tasks that once required your time, this distinction becomes more important. When messages can be generated quickly, responses drafted for you, and scheduling handled automatically, it changes how much effort is required to stay in contact with people.

At first, that may feel like an advantage. You can communicate more efficiently and keep up with more people in less time. Over time, something else begins to change. When interaction becomes easier, it also becomes easier to move through it without fully engaging.

You may find yourself responding without thinking as much about what the other person actually needs. You may move from one conversation to the next without giving any of them your full attention. The volume of interaction increases, yet the depth begins to decrease.

When that happens, connection starts to lose its role in how you experience meaning.

That does not mean connection disappears. It means you have to become more aware of when something real is happening. When machines can handle the mechanics of communication, the value shifts to what cannot be automated. The difference comes from how present you are, how well you understand the other person, and whether something actually changes for them.

For someone who finds meaning through connection, this becomes a choice rather than something that happens automatically. You begin to notice which interactions feel different and why. You recognize the moments where something shifts and the ones where it does not.

That awareness begins to change how you use your time.

Instead of trying to have more conversations, you begin paying attention to the ones that have impact. You notice when someone leaves the conversation seeing something differently. You recognize when something stands out to you afterward.

You may also notice that impact does not require a long conversation. A brief interaction can be more impactful than a long one if something shifts. What matters is not how long you talked, but whether something changed.

When you begin to approach your interactions this way, your day starts to feel different. You are not measuring it by how many conversations you had or how much you accomplished through them. You are paying attention to which moments made a difference and how they influenced the rest of your day.

That shift changes how you use your time.

If your current work includes opportunities for meaningful connection, you begin to recognize them more clearly. You may choose to stay in certain conversations longer, follow up on interactions that felt different, and approach discussions with more focus because you understand what creates that sense of impact for you.

If your work does not naturally provide those moments, or if you are not working in the same way, you begin to create them yourself. That might mean choosing to stay present when something begins to shift, asking a question that helps someone see things differently, or simply not rushing past a moment that feels important.

You begin to see that connection is not limited to specific roles or settings. It can happen in everyday interactions when you are paying attention to what actually changes for the other person.

There are also signals that help you recognize when connection is working in the way that creates meaning for you. You may notice yourself thinking about a conversation later without effort, or realize that something about the interaction changed how you see a situation. You can tell the conversation did not end the same way it started.

Another signal is how your attention behaves during the conversation. In routine exchanges, your attention can drift. In meaningful ones, it is easier to stay focused. You are not thinking about what comes next or what you need to say. You are fully engaged with the person in front of you, and that changes the quality of the interaction.

If you are not sure where to begin, it helps to slow down in situations where you would normally move quickly. Instead of responding immediately, you allow a moment to understand what is actually being said. You listen for what is behind the words, not just the words themselves. That small shift can change how the interaction develops.

Over time, these small adjustments begin to build. Your interactions start to feel more connected, and your days feel less fragmented because certain moments stay with you beyond the conversation itself. You begin to recognize which interactions carry forward and which ones fade.

You are no longer moving from one conversation to the next without noticing the difference. You start to see when something changes for the other person, even in small ways, and those moments stand out more clearly.

That is when you begin to understand how connection shapes your time. It is not based on how many interactions you have, but on whether something shifts in a way that continues beyond the moment.

And once you recognize that, your attention naturally begins to move toward those moments, because you can feel the difference when something real happens between you and someone else.

CHAPTER 23

Creation

Your day might start with an idea that will not leave you alone because it feels like it could turn into something if you gave it time. It might be a sentence, a concept, a problem you want to solve, or something that could be improved. You tell yourself you will think about it for a few minutes, jot something down, and then move on, but that is not what happens.

One thought leads to another and before long you are in deep. You are writing, building, outlining, organizing, or shaping something that did not exist an hour ago. You forget what you had originally planned for your day because you are following the idea as it develops, moving between details and the bigger picture without forcing either one.

At some point, you look up and realize how much time has passed. You are so focused that stopping does not occur to you. When you look at what you have, there is something there. It may not be finished or perfect, but it exists. You can recognize it and pick up where you left off.

That is what changes how your time feels.

Some days blur together even when you are busy. Other days come down to one thing you spent hours on. You may not have finished it, but you know exactly what you did and where you left off. The difference is not how much you completed. It is whether your effort led to something that is now there because of you.

Meaning for creators develops when your ideas and time turn into something that is there because of you. You can return to it and keep developing it, but it does not necessarily require perfection or completion. It simply requires that the effort you put into developing something leads to some form.

When that happens, your day has a different kind of structure. You are not moving from one task to another with nothing connecting them. You are building something that has meaning. Even when you stop working on it, it serves as a form of creative expression that you can always go back to if you want.

That sense of continuation is what gives creation its meaning.

You begin with an idea that feels unfinished and uncertain. As you work through it, parts come together and others fall apart. But you can adjust, move pieces around, and test what holds up. You may pause because something is not clear, and when you return, you see what you missed and keep going. Each time you return to it, you learn something else from it that provides a boost to your day.

Over time, that process begins to shape how you see yourself. You are not just someone who has ideas. You are someone who turns them into something that can be seen, used, or built on. That identity goes beyond a moment and builds each time you take something that did not exist and give it form.

You also notice when that part of your experience is missing.

You can spend an entire day responding to messages, attending meetings, and completing what is expected, yet something feels off. You stayed busy, but there is nothing you can point to that exists because of your effort. Without that, even a full day can feel like it did not lead anywhere.

That contrast becomes easier to recognize once you have experienced both sides. You begin to see that activity alone does not create meaning for you. Movement between tasks does not create it either. It comes from building something that remains after you stop working on it, even if it is not physical.

That changes the things you pay attention to during your day.

Instead of only focusing on what needs to be done next, you begin to notice which ideas hold your attention long enough to become something more. You recognize when you are in the middle of creating because your focus stays steady. You are not thinking about what comes next. You are working through what is in front of you until it takes clearer form.

That focus feels different from routine work. It is not about speed or efficiency. It is about progress you can see. Even small movement matters because it changes what exists. A paragraph becomes a page. A rough outline becomes something you can follow. A partial solution becomes something that works.

Those changes accumulate.

You may not notice them in the moment, but when you step back, you can see that your time led somewhere. That is what allows you to return and continue without starting over. The work carries forward because it exists outside of your immediate attention.

When that does not happen, your time can simply reset more easily. When you are not creating, you move from one task to the next, completing what is required, and then moving on again. That can leave you feeling like something is missing, especially if nothing really changed due to your efforts.

As intelligent machines take on more of the tasks that once required your time, this distinction becomes more important. You can complete whatever is left of your work without engaging deeply in the process of creating.

At first, that may feel efficient. You can produce more in less time and move on to the next thing quickly. Over time, that can lead you to lose the sense that your effort led to something.

You may find yourself reviewing, editing, or approving rather than building. You may move from one output to another without feeling connected to what was created. The volume of your work can increase, yet your sense of meaning can decrease.

That is when creation starts to lose its role in how you experience your time. But it does not disappear. It becomes something you have to be more intentional about.

When machines can assist with producing outcomes, the value you receive changes based on how you engage in the process. The difference comes from whether you are involved in shaping what exists or simply moving through what has already been formed. Creation, for you, comes from being part of the work that gives something its form.

That awareness gives you a way to shape your time.

Instead of only focusing on what needs to be completed, you begin to notice where your effort leads to something that continues. You recognize which work leaves something behind that you can return to and which work fades once it is done.

You may also notice that creation does not require large blocks of time. A small amount of focused effort can lead to something that changes what exists. What matters is not how long you worked, but whether something is now there that was not there before.

That perspective changes how you approach your day.

You begin to value progress you can see, even if it is incomplete. You are more likely to spend a little more time on something than you normally would so it can move forward rather than shifting too quickly to something else. You recognize that stopping too early often means losing the continuity that gives the work its meaning.

When you approach your time this way, your day begins to feel different. You are not measuring it by how many tasks you completed or how busy you were. You are paying attention to what now exists because of your effort and how it can be continued.

That shift changes how you use your time.

If your current work includes opportunities to create, you begin to recognize them more clearly. You may choose to spend more time on certain projects, come back to them more consistently, or protect time where you can focus without interruption. You understand that those moments are what allow something to take shape.

If your work does not naturally provide those opportunities, you can begin to create them yourself. That might mean setting aside time to build something that matters to you, even if it is not required. It might mean taking an existing task and engaging with it more deeply so that your effort leads to something you can see and continue.

You begin to see that creation is not limited to specific roles or outcomes. It can happen in any context where your effort results in something that exists beyond the moment you worked on it.

There are also signals that help you recognize when creation is working in the way that creates meaning for you.

You can return to what you worked on without starting over. You gain meaning in seeing what comes next. When you see evidence of progress, even if it is small, you feel a sense that your time is connected because each session builds on the last.

Another signal is how your attention behaves while you are working. In routine tasks, your focus can drift. In creative work, your attention stays with what you are building. You are engaged with the process itself, not just the outcome.

If you are not sure where to begin, it helps to work on something slightly longer than you normally would. Instead of stopping when it is partially formed, you continue until there is a clearer structure. You allow time for the idea to take shape rather than moving on too quickly.

That small change can impact how you derive meaning from your work.

Over time, these small adjustments begin to build. Your days feel less fragmented because your time is contributing to something that continues.

You are no longer moving from one task to the next without noticing the difference. You begin to recognize when your effort leads to something that remains, even if it is still unfinished.

Those moments stand out because they give your time a sense of continuity.

That is when you begin to understand how creation shapes your time. It is not based on how much you complete, but on whether something now exists that you can return to and continue building.

And once you recognize that, your attention naturally begins to move toward the work that allows something to take form, because you can see and feel the difference when your effort leads to something that lasts.

CHAPTER 24

Influence

If your day involves being part of a team, you likely have experienced a time when some problem that kept everything stuck got solved. The longer the problem persisted, the better it felt to resolve it. Sometimes that comes from something as simple as a clarifying question that reframes the issue for everyone. When people's perception of an issue or perspective changes, what might have seemed insurmountable now suddenly feels doable.

You have likely experienced smaller versions of that in your own day. It might be something as simple as a decision that seemed out of reach and suddenly becomes easier to decide. Or a group that was unsure but now becomes aligned around what to do next. In the moment, it may not feel dramatic, yet something changed in a way that would not have happened otherwise.

When you look back on those situations, you notice that someone in the group did something that changed the outcome. And if you trace it back, you can often connect that shift to something that was said, asked, or contributed by them. When that happens, the person who made that impact often finds their influence provided them with meaning.

Influence creates meaning when your input impacts others in teams, groups, and communities. You do not have to say much, but your involvement can contribute to the changes that happen next.

Those moments do not always stand out to you right away. You may move on to the next task or conversation without thinking much about it. Later, you recognize that something improved in a way it had not before. That realization is often when the impact you made becomes clear.

You do not have to direct or control everything that happens. You might just be part of a moment where something shifts, and that shift changes the outcome for the group. Even when it is subtle, you can see that the direction would have been different without your involvement.

Once you begin to notice that, it becomes easier to understand why some interactions feel more meaningful than others. You can participate in many conversations without anything changing. They move forward, decisions get made, and work continues, yet your involvement does not affect the outcome in a noticeable way.

Other times, a single contribution changes how people think, decide, or act. That difference is easy to recognize when you look back on it. That is what separates participation from influence.

There is often a brief moment before you speak where you sense that what you say could shift things. It is not always comfortable. You may hesitate because you are not sure how your point will land, or whether it will interrupt the flow of the discussion. You know speaking up could potentially be the solution everyone has been looking for, or your input might just as easily be ignored. But, for those of you who value influence, you speak up anyway.

When you recognize it and choose to step in, you are not trying to control the outcome. You are responding to the sense that something could change. When it does, it is rarely because of a long explanation. It is usually something simple, said at the right time, that allows others to see the situation differently.

In moments where your input has an effect, you are listening for where things are unclear, where assumptions are being made, or where a different perspective could change direction. You are not trying to speak more. You are paying attention to when your contribution will matter.

When a shift happens, it impacts how the group responds. Someone builds on what was said, a decision becomes clearer, and the next step is easier to identify. The conversation makes progress in a way that was not happening before.

Those changes do not need to be acknowledged because you can see them in what happens next.

Over time, these moments begin to shape how you see your role. You recognize that your perspective, your timing, and your willingness to step in can influence what happens around you. That recognition builds as those moments repeat.

You also notice when that element is missing.

You can be involved in discussions, contribute ideas, and stay engaged, yet nothing changes because of your involvement. The conversation continues without shifting direction. Decisions are made, but your input did not alter the outcome. That experience feels different, even when the work itself is similar.

That contrast helps you understand where influence creates meaning for you.

You cannot be involved in every decision, but when you are involved, you can recognize when your contribution impacts what happens next and choose to engage in those moments.

Influence impacts many different settings. It can happen in leadership roles, in communities, in teams, or in informal groups where no one has formal authority. The common thread is not the position you hold. It is whether your presence changes the direction things take.

As intelligent machines take on more of the work that supports decision-making, this distinction becomes more important. The output they create can make it easier for groups to move forward without much discussion.

At the same time, it can make it harder to recognize where human input can be the most important thing to change direction.

When recommendations are generated and decisions are supported by systems, it is easy to follow what is presented without questioning it. Conversations can become shorter, and decisions can appear more straightforward.

That is where influence needs to become more intentional.

You can experience it when you question an assumption, reframe an issue, or point out something that has been overlooked. You can also make a meaningful impact when you recognize that the direction being taken is not the only option and offer an alternative that changes how people think about the situation.

Those contributions do not replace the information that is available, but they do change how it is used.

As that becomes clearer, you notice how your influence impacts outcomes. That awareness shapes how you engage with others.

That determines how selective you are about stepping in and makes you more aware of how your input affects what happens next. You recognize that one well-timed contribution can impact more than many smaller ones that do not change anything.

You may also notice that influence does not require long discussions. A brief question or a single point can be enough to shift how people see something. What matters is not the length of the interaction, but whether it changes the outcome.

When you begin to approach your time this way, your day feels different.

You are not measuring it by how much you contributed or how visible your role was. You are paying attention to where your involvement changed what happened next and how those moments shaped outcomes. That shift changes how you use your time.

If your current work includes opportunities to influence in this way, you begin to recognize them more clearly. You may step into certain discussions more intentionally or choose to contribute when you see an opportunity to shift direction.

If your work does not naturally provide those moments, you begin to create them by paying attention to where your input can make a difference. That might mean asking a question that changes how people think about a problem or offering a perspective that opens a different path forward.

You begin to see that influence is not tied to a title or formal authority. It comes from how your input affects what happens within a group.

There are also signals that help you recognize when influence is working in the way that creates meaning for you.

You can connect a change in direction to something you contributed, see that the outcome would have been different without your involvement, or notice that people respond to what you say in a way that moves things forward.

Another signal is how the group behaves after you contribute. You might see that conversations become clearer, decisions are made more easily, and the next steps become more defined. Those changes show that your input affected what happened next.

If you are not sure where to begin, it helps to pay attention to moments where things feel unclear or stalled. Instead of moving past them, you consider whether something you say could help shift direction. You do not need to force it. You simply become more aware of when your input can have an effect.

Over time, these moments begin to accumulate.

You start to recognize patterns in where your influence is strongest and where it is not. That recognition helps you see more clearly when your input changes what happens next and when it does not.

You are no longer participating without noticing the difference. You begin to see when a conversation shifts because of something you said or asked, even in small ways, and those moments stand out more clearly.

That is when you begin to understand how influence shapes your time. It is not based on how much you contribute, but on whether your involvement changes direction in a way that continues beyond the moment.

And once you recognize that, your attention naturally begins to move toward those moments, because you can feel the difference when your input changes what happens next.

CHAPTER 25

Intelligent Machines and the Four Paths

While knowing the paths that inspire you is helpful, meaning is something you keep working at. No one can hand you a formula that guarantees you'll find it. Intelligent machines may have played a role in taking away some of the meaning you experienced, and at the same time they may be part of what helps you discover more of it. They can answer a lot, but they can't tell you what matters to you. What you have discovered is an awareness of what inspires you, whether it's chasing ideas, building something meaningful, connecting in a real way, or influencing outcomes. The question now is: How do you use these intelligent machines to amplify that, instead of holding you back?

That question becomes even more important now because intelligent machines have worked their way into so many parts of your life. They sort information, draft ideas, answer questions, summarize meetings, compare options, organize projects, and save time across almost everything you do. That can feel exciting, threatening, useful, distracting, or all of those at once. It can also create a kind of pressure, because the same technology that may reduce certain kinds of work also leaves you with more responsibility for how you decide what to do with your time each day.

That is where the four paths become useful in a different way. They give you a way to think about how to use intelligent machines without getting pulled into passive activity, empty efficiency, or constant distraction. The goal is to understand how these tools can support the parts of your life that already give you energy, purpose, and direction.

Exploration

If you feel drawn to exploration, intelligent machines can be incredibly useful because they make it easier to follow a question while building on your curiosity. Years ago, you could become interested in something and lose that interest before you found enough information to do anything useful with it. You might have needed a stack of books, a trip to a library, or far more time than your schedule allowed. Now you can begin with a question and get far more than an explanation. You can get a comparison, disagreement, context, and background all in the blink of an eye.

That changes the experience of learning, and it changes it in a way that can be deeply satisfying for someone who gains meaning through understanding. A person like that usually wants more than a quick answer. That person wants to know where the answer came from, what the weak spots are, what other people think, what the hidden assumptions may be, and what that actually means beyond the obvious answer. Intelligent machines can support that by making it easier to keep going. You can ask for the basic explanation, then the business angle, then the social angle, then the historical angle, then the strongest opposing view, and then the practical implications in your own life.

You can use that at work, and you can use it outside of work too. If you are trying to understand a new subject, learn your way around a field, examine a complicated issue, compare several directions, or make sense of a question that has been sitting in the back of your mind, the machine can help you build a better starting point. It can define unfamiliar language, suggest what to read next, explain why people disagree, and help you see what the first answer leaves out. It doesn't replace your thinking; it just gives you more to work with.

At the same time, this is also where people can lose themselves fastest. Intelligent machines make it very easy to bounce from one idea to the next, and that can feel productive while leaving you with very little to show for it. A person can spend two hours asking one interesting question after another and end the day with a head full of fragments and no real understanding. For someone who gains meaning through exploration, the better use of the tool comes from choosing a question that has a clear purpose and spending time with the information you gather so you can see what actually leads somewhere meaningful.

When you do that, it turns your curiosity into a search for understanding instead of jumping from one thing to another. It can help you examine your assumptions and begin forming a point of view that is actually yours. Once that happens, exploration starts affecting how you spend your day, and that's where the experience actually starts to mean something.

Connection

Intelligent machines can build your sense of connection by making communication easier. When they are used too heavily, though, they can also make communication feel meaningless. You can send more messages, respond faster, and stay in contact with more people than ever before and still feel lonely by the end of the day. That is why connection has never really been about volume. It has always been about whether another person feels heard, understood, supported, respected, or changed by the interaction.

That is where these tools can be surprisingly helpful when used well. They can help you think through a difficult message before you send it, sort out wording that feels harsher than you intended, organize your thoughts before a conversation that carries emotional issues, or help you speak more clearly when you care about the relationship enough to want to get it right. That can actually improve your connection because it helps you respond more clearly and with more care.

It can also help you prepare for conversations that people often avoid even when they care deeply about the outcome. You may need to reconnect with someone after too much silence, respond to disappointment without making the situation worse, offer support to someone who is struggling, or speak honestly in a relationship that feels strained. Intelligent machines can help you think through what you want to say and how to say it in a way that sounds like you. That can lower the barrier that often keeps people from interacting when a relationship would benefit from a little courage and someone actually showing they care.

These tools can also help you become more thoughtful in the way you listen. You can use them to generate stronger questions before a conversation, think through what someone else may be experiencing, or prepare for differences in age, culture, profession, or personality that affect the way people hear each other. That preparation can strengthen a conversation because you arrive with more awareness and stop relying so much on your assumptions.

Intelligent machines can support your thinking, but your presence is what carries the interaction. People can feel the difference between a message that is clear and a message that is polished into something smooth and empty. They know when there is a real person in the room and when there is language that sounds arranged and detached. The better way to use it is to let it help you prepare, then step back and let your own voice carry the message.

Creation

Creation brings another level of complexity because intelligent machines can produce material so quickly that many people confuse output with meaning. A person who gains meaning through creation usually cares about more than seeing something appear on a screen. That person cares about bringing an idea into form, shaping it, improving it, and seeing a real result take shape through effort and judgment. The machine can help with that process, and it can also cheapen it if you use it to create everything for you.

One of the best uses of these tools in creation comes at the beginning, when ideas are still rough and difficult to envision. Many people lose momentum because they get stuck with an idea in their head and the first step feels too big to take. Intelligent machines can help you break things into steps you can actually work through by helping with structure, sequence, options, and early drafts. They can give you something to react to, refine, cut, combine, reject, or improve. That can keep the creative process alive when you might have otherwise shelved your idea.

Creation goes way beyond writing. It can help with business-related presentations, courses, workshops, and many other things to improve how you do your work. But it can also be artistic and help with comedy, music, art, and other personal creative aspects. If you gain meaning through creation, intelligent machines can support you by helping get your idea out of your head and into an actual form.

A lot of the real value comes when you start revising. You can compare versions, identify repetition, find weak spots, improve structure, or test whether the piece is saying what you want it to say. That kind of help can strengthen your standards rather than weaken them if you keep your judgment fully involved. You are still the one deciding what belongs, what sounds right, what carries your voice, and what deserves to stay.

It's important to recognize that the speed at which these systems operate can make you settle on a suggestion too quickly. They often generate something that looks finished and then you accept it just because it exists, even though it carries very little value, thought, or care. For someone who gains meaning through creation, that shortcut stops feeling satisfying pretty quickly. Real meaning comes from shaping something until it reflects your choices, your taste, your standards, and your sense of what is worth sharing.

Influence

When you are drawn to being an influential part of a team, group, or community, intelligent machines can provide summaries, proposals, polished language, and persuasive framing with very little effort. That is why your judgment is even more important. When many people have access to the same smooth wording, the difference comes from your perspective on an issue, asking the question that helps a group think more clearly, and offering a point of view that people trust enough to follow.

This is where intelligent machines can strengthen the preparation part of the process without replacing the conviction you bring. They can help you organize your thoughts before a difficult conversation, sharpen a recommendation, anticipate concerns, compare versions of an argument, or clarify the strongest evidence behind your position. That kind of support can make a real difference because it allows you to enter a room with a clearer idea of what needs to be said and why.

That is useful in business, family life, leadership, education, community work, and almost any setting where other people are involved in a decision. You may need to raise a concern before a group heads in the wrong direction, explain a proposal more clearly, or help people understand the consequences of an easy but unwise choice. Intelligent machines can help you think that through more carefully. They can help you prepare for what may be misunderstood and strengthen the way you frame your point.

With everything machines can do, you still have to supply the courage. Real influence has always depended on judgment, timing, integrity, and the willingness to speak when speaking carries some risk. The tool can support your preparation, but the human part of influence still comes from you.

The Four Paths

When you look at the four paths, you don't have to see intelligent machines as something that get in the way of finding meaning. You can use the machines in a way that supports the parts of your life that already give you purpose. The challenge is making sure they don't turn into a distraction and instead become a useful way to improve learning, stronger relationships, better work, and more thoughtful decisions.

You can fill a day with activity and still feel like you didn't really get anywhere. You can also use the same tools to think more clearly, have better conversations, and do more meaningful work. The difference comes down to how you use them. You already have a clearer sense of what actually matters to you, and this is where that starts to show in how you spend your time.

The tools can help, but the direction still comes from you. You can use these systems to go deeper into the things that actually mean something to you, or you can spend your time reacting to whatever they make easy. One of those leads somewhere. The other just fills the day.

PART VI

A New Form of Contribution

CHAPTER 26

What Changes Over Time

There is a point where something begins to change, and you may not notice it right away. Up until now, most of what you have been working through has centered on you – what holds you back, what interests you, and what gives your day meaning. That focus is important because if you do not understand what drives you, it becomes difficult to create a life that feels worthwhile. Over time, though, the way you experience that effort begins to change.

That is how it started for me. I was always fascinated by curiosity, but I never considered that it could lead to something more. After interviewing thousands of people on my radio show, I began to see that some guests were more interesting than others, and it was not just because of what they had accomplished. It was how they thought, how they asked questions, and how they approached the world.

I kept coming back to that, and it made me want to understand what was behind it. That is what led me to write about curiosity in the first place. At that time, I was not thinking about anything beyond understanding it for myself. I was following something that caught my attention and spending time with it because it felt worth it.

I did not expect how that would evolve. The work eventually led to the creation of the Curiosity Code Index®, which became the first assessment designed to determine what inhibits curiosity. That came from continuing to explore something that held my attention. It was not planned as anything larger. It developed because I spent enough time on it to see where it would go.

For a long time, I did not see myself as a creative person. When I thought about creativity, I pictured someone artistic, someone who could sing, paint, or come up with something unusual on demand. That did not feel like me. What I was doing felt more like trying to understand something that did not make sense. I kept asking why people felt stuck and what was getting in their way, and that led me to start asking people directly. Once I saw the patterns in what they shared, it raised another question for me. Why was no one doing anything about it?

That is where things started to change in a way I did not expect. I had studied assessments when I wrote my dissertation on emotional intelligence, so I understood how they worked. What I did not see at the time was that I was moving from trying to understand something into creating something from it. I was still following the same line of questioning, but it began to take form in a different way. Only later did I realize that what I had been doing all along was a form of creativity; it just did not look like what I had always assumed creativity had to be.

As that happened, something else changed as well. The meaning I took from the work no longer came only from understanding it or building something around it. It began to come from what I could see happening as a result of staying engaged with it over time. That change did not happen all at once, and it was not something I was trying to create. It was something I only recognized later.

Many people do not see this right away. Early on, meaning is tied closely to what you are doing. You focus on learning, building, and figuring things out because that is what keeps you engaged. Over time, the source of that meaning begins to feel different. It becomes less about what you are accomplishing for yourself and more about how you experience what you are doing as you continue.

When you look back at the four paths, you can see how this develops without needing to force it. If you are drawn to exploration, what you spend time learning starts to make more sense the more time you spend with it. If you are drawn to creation, what you build begins to feel more substantial because it continues beyond the time you spent working on it. If you are drawn to connection, certain interactions stand out in a way they did not before because of how they felt rather than what was said. And if you are drawn to influence, the moments where your input made a difference become clearer to you when you reflect on them later.

None of that requires anything formal, and it does not depend on recognition or visibility. It develops as you keep spending time on it. As you continue to engage with what draws you, you start to see which moments you keep thinking about later and which ones you do not. That difference becomes more important than any external marker because it reflects what your time actually feels like.

You may find that what once felt important does not hold the same level of interest anymore. You may also find that things you did not pay much attention to before begin to stand out more. It happens as you spend more time with what fits you.

There is also a change in how you evaluate your time. Earlier, progress is often measured by what you complete or achieve. Later, it becomes easier to recognize when something is worth continuing and when it is not. That does not mean achievement stops being important. It means it is no longer the only way you understand the value of what you are doing.

This becomes especially noticeable when structure is less defined. In the past, roles and expectations made it easier to understand how your time was being used. As those structures change, that clarity is not always there. What replaces it is your own sense of what is worth continuing, based on what you have experienced over time.

At some point, it becomes clear that what is important to you is not exactly the same as it was before. The way you experience what your effort produces begins to change, and that becomes a more reliable guide than anything external.

If you step back and look at your own life, you can likely see this already. There are things you used to focus on that no longer hold your attention in the same way, and there are other things that have become more important without you trying to make them that way. That change is not something you plan. It develops as you continue to engage with what fits you.

When what is important to you starts to change, it becomes clearer where you want to focus your effort, based on what you have already experienced.

That awareness becomes more useful than any single decision. You are not trying to map everything out ahead of time. You pay attention to what has already proven worth your effort and use that to guide what you do next.

Over time, you start to see the difference in how you spend your days and the choices you make.

CHAPTER 27

The Noisy TV Problem

If you have ever heard the phrase Noisy TV problem, it stems from research out of Berkeley. This is the same line of research I mentioned earlier when discussing artificial curiosity, where researchers wanted to see if AI could develop behavior driven by curiosity rather than goals. Most computer programs were traditionally rewarded for achieving goals or solving problems. In this case, the researchers decided to flip that idea and reward the program for being surprised.

The AI agent was placed inside a video game environment, and instead of being told to win, it was rewarded whenever it encountered something it could not predict. That way of working was new to the system, and it kept trying to predict what would happen next, but when it stayed in familiar territory and made accurate predictions, instead of receiving a reward, its rewards were reduced. When it explored something new and its predictions were wrong, the reward increased. That might sound strange, but it was how they thought it would encourage behavior that would be more like curiosity, where the system would seek out what surprised it. And it worked for a while. The agent began to explore more of the game's environment, moving through levels and discovering new areas without ever being told to do so.

Just as the researchers began to think they created artificial curiosity, something unexpected happened. The system discovered a shortcut that allowed it to maximize its reward without actually learning anything meaningful. Instead of continuing to explore the environment in useful ways, it found something that constantly surprised it without requiring effort or progress.

This is known as the Noisy TV problem. If you have ever seen a television tuned into static, every frame looks slightly unpredictable because it is constantly changing. From the system's perspective, this was a perfect place to remain because it figured it could not predict what came next, which means it could generate endless rewards. It beat the system. The problem is that the AI never discovered anything meaningful. It was just stuck consuming nonsense that, although appearing as novelty, delivered no value.

That taught the world something deeper about curiosity. Curiosity without direction can potentially lead nowhere; like how people spend their time now, moving from one screen to another, scrolling, clicking, watching, and constantly shifting attention. There is always something new, always something different, and like the static on the TV, always something that grabs attention for a moment, but lacks depth.

Many of us can go through an entire day consuming new information and still feel like it never led to anything productive or meaningful. That is our human version of the Noisy TV problem. We are doing things, but those things lack direction and purpose behind just keeping busy. As the novelty wears off for us, our sense of meaning can begin to fade.

As I started thinking about what this could look like in the future, I realized there are two completely different scenarios: We can either work alongside intelligent machines and use our adaptive curiosity to figure out how to keep developing, or we could get to a place where intelligent machines completely replace human involvement in the workplace. This may not happen overnight, and it may not happen at all. If you listen to people like Elon Musk, work might be optional, and it's not as far off as many of us might think.

If and when that happens, what do you do with your day when no one tells you what your day should look like? You know from previous chapters and your own experience that work has always provided structure, whether people enjoyed it or not. It gave you a reason to get up, a place to go, and a way to measure progress. When that structure disappears, the absence of it becomes noticeable very quickly.

Just like for a new retiree, more free time sounds appealing at first, and many people imagine filling that time with leisure activities. Some will do exactly that and feel satisfied. I imagine some of you are thinking, I'll just play golf. That's fine as long as it makes you happy. But in this kind of future, there's still no clear answer for how people will pay for things. Golf might be off the table for many of us. And others might find that leisure alone does not provide a sense of meaning. The difference between being busy and feeling fulfilled becomes much more obvious when there is no external structure guiding your choices.

That's when you start to run the risk of the Noisy TV problem. Without a way to direct your curiosity, you might naturally gravitate toward whatever is easiest and most immediately stimulating. As you consume "static," you spend less time on creation and other activities that could make you feel more engaged with your life.

If jobs are gone, your time will be unstructured, and you will need to be the one to determine how to design a new structure for your day. That's when I started thinking about a different approach. For the sake of thinking it through, humor me for a moment and picture where instead of relying on your job to structure your time, you had somewhere else to go that included a new and different kind of structure. Let's call those locations hubs. Basically, they could be places that used to be office buildings or even a virtual space that would be different from going to work because there would be no compensation.

They could be environments designed around four key drivers of meaning you learned about earlier, which include exploration, creation, connection, and influence.

The hubs could be places where you go to learn, discover, and investigate ideas that interest you. These could include research spaces, learning labs, and collaborative environments where people work through questions and experiment with new concepts. Hubs could also be focused on building and producing tangible things. These could include inventor spaces, studios, or incubators where people bring ideas to life. The emphasis would be on progress, experimentation, and iteration. You would not be creating for someone other than the community, necessarily, but you could be. You could also just be working on something that matters to you.

The hubs would provide a sense of connection because they would center around relationships and shared experiences. Some of them could include group discussions, mentorship opportunities, and collaborative projects that bring people together.

There wouldn't necessarily be four different kinds of hubs for each of those pathways, because many of the experiences overlap. However, in that reality, you could pick and choose the things that interest you most and move between experiences throughout the day. You might spend part of your day exploring an idea, then move into a creation space to build something related to it, and later join a group discussion to share what you learned. That kind of flow is how people naturally engage when things matter to them.

It would be your choice whether you wanted to engage with these interconnected hubs, which would avoid any siloed information, just like the Internet is available to everyone. I envision something like senior communities or cruise ships where certain hours of the day are more structured for people who like that. The most important thing is that no one would be required to participate.

I intentionally have not made predictions in this book because everything changes so quickly. Also, I initially hesitated to suggest this or any other reality as a potential future, because of the political and governmental aspects that would need to be addressed. I am not a Pollyanna-like person who expects a perfect utopian future. Having grown up in the United States, I have always been around a capitalistic society, and one that prefers less government involvement. Something like a hub-based system would require a lot of development in terms of infrastructure and design, which would take years to develop. That likely would require more government involvement. That would not be popular with many of you. Losing the capitalism-based culture would also be a major issue.

There are some very real challenges that come with this idea. Who would pay for it if not the government? There would also be challenges related to how people adapt to having more control over their time. Many people are used to having structure provided for them, and designing their own day requires a different level of awareness and discipline.

This is not a simple solution, and it would not be easy to implement. It requires a shift in how people think about work, time, and meaning, and the goal would still be to direct your time in a way that feels meaningful. For me, this was simply an exercise in adaptive curiosity, a way to think through one possible future. With adaptive curiosity, things change every day, and this idea might not make any sense at all if jobs remain relatively stable. I offer this to give you something to react to, to encourage you to imagine a better future that leads to meaning, and to invite you to share your own ideas the way I've shared mine, because the real value comes from exploring possibilities together and moving toward something that works.

This is just one of many ideas that could lead to finding meaning someday. It also raises a bigger question about what we will value if work no longer defines our time. I often think about the movie, *In Time*, with Justin Timberlake, where time is the new currency instead of money. In that world, people stop aging at 25, but they only get one extra year of life on a digital clock embedded in their arm. Time is literally money. You earn it, spend it, or run out and die, which forces every decision to be tied directly to what something is worth.

If intelligent machines begin handling what humans once did, the way value is defined may begin to change as well. If money is no longer tied to effort in the same way, something else may take its place as the measure of what matters. It could be contribution, creation, or simply how you choose to engage with the world and how you spend your time in ways that feel meaningful.

The idea of hubs is simply one way to think through what might be possible. It is not a prediction, and it is not meant to suggest that this is the direction things should go in. It is just an attempt to consider what people might need if the structure that has guided their lives begins to change.

What matters more than the specific solution is that this is a question worth thinking about now. If the way you spend your time changes, then how you create meaning has to change with it. That is not something to wait for and figure out later. As I've told my students in my Foresight in Technology course, you look ahead and work backward from there. However this plays out, the real issue is how you avoid drifting into your own version of the Noisy TV problem and instead direct your curiosity toward something that builds, connects, and contributes.

CHAPTER 28

Preparing Future Generations

I have been thinking a lot about what the world will look like for people who are just getting started, and in my case, that has become very personal because I now have two grandchildren, one still a toddler and the other just a baby. When I look at them, it is hard not to wonder what their daily lives will look like when they are older, what they will wake up to each day, and how they will decide what to do with their time in a world that may not resemble the one most of us have known.

That is what makes this moment feel different from past transitions. People have always adapted to change, and every generation has faced its own version of uncertainty, yet there has usually been a foundation people could return to, something that provided a sense of stability even as things changed around it. What is emerging now feels less anchored, and that can be difficult if you are used to having a clear path in front of you. The path is no longer marked the way it used to be, and that requires a different way of thinking.

When I think about my grandchildren, I do not think about what specific jobs they will have or what industries will exist by the time they enter the workforce, because that is almost impossible to predict. What I think about instead is how they will learn to make decisions when there is no clear answer, how they will handle days when there is no structure telling them what matters, and how they will create a sense of meaning in a world that may no longer provide it. These questions feel much more important than any specific skill they might learn along the way.

When you think about the people who are coming next, whether that is your own children, grandchildren, students, or anyone you influence, they are not going to learn how to navigate this kind of world from instructions alone. They are going to learn from what they see, from how you respond to uncertainty, from how you handle situations where there is no clear answer, and from how you decide what matters when no one is telling you what to prioritize. That puts you in a different kind of position, because you must figure out your own direction.

That can feel like a lot to carry, especially when you consider that most of us have not experienced this kind of environment ourselves. We were not trained to operate without structure. We were trained to follow it, to work within it, and to measure ourselves against it. Now, you are being asked to move beyond that, and at the same time, help others learn how to do the same thing.

If you look at how people actually become more capable in uncertain situations, it comes from trying something, seeing what happens, and realizing that they can handle what comes next. That experience builds a kind of confidence that comes from experience, not certainty, because it is based on having moved through something rather than having predicted it in advance. Over time, that becomes more useful than any set of instructions, because it allows someone to keep going even when there is no clear direction.

That is why this is not just a personal exercise. It extends beyond you in ways that are easy to underestimate. When you find meaning through exploration, you show others what it looks like to stay curious and engaged with the world. When you find meaning through connection, you demonstrate the value of being present with other people in a way that goes beyond surface interaction. When you find meaning through creation, you show that building something, even something small, can give your time direction. When you find meaning through influence, you make it clear that your actions can shape outcomes in ways that matter.

Those are visible behaviors, and they are the things people notice, even when you are not trying to teach anything. If you think about your own experiences growing up, you can probably remember people who influenced how you think today, even if they never set out to do that. What you remember is not a set of instructions, but how they approached things, how they responded to challenges, and how they engaged with the world around them. That is what you are doing now.

When I think about my grandchildren, I do not feel pressure to give them a perfect road map, because that is not something I can provide and not something they will need in the same way previous generations did. What matters more is helping them develop the ability to engage with whatever is in front of them, to stay curious, to try things, and to build a sense of meaning that is not dependent on someone else telling them what it should be. That is not something you wait to teach. It is something you demonstrate in how you approach your own life.

As you continue from here, the question is not whether the world will continue to change. It will. The question is how you will respond to that change, and how that response will influence the people around you. You do not need to have everything figured out to do that well. You need to be willing to engage, try, adjust, and continue even when things are not clear, because that is what allows you to build a life that feels meaningful in a way that is not dependent on a fixed direction.

If there is one thing to carry forward, it is this. Meaning is not something you wait to find. It is something you build through how you engage with your time, your choices, and the people around you. When you take that seriously, it changes how you experience your own life, and it changes what you make possible for the people who are coming next, which is what will matter most long after any specific direction has changed.

Conclusion

Any book on curiosity should leave you with more questions than answers. With every book I have written, it has led me to questions I had never considered before I started.

For this book, one question kept coming back to me. I kept thinking about the Noisy TV problem. I wanted to know if they solved it and, more important, how they solved it. If researchers could change behavior in a system that kept getting stuck in meaningless noise, I wanted to understand what they actually did and whether any of that could help us as humans.

What they did was surprisingly practical. They changed what the system counted as a reward. The system gained strength when it focused on something it could learn from and use again, staying with it long enough for one step to lead into another. Over time, that single adjustment shaped what the system returned to and what it ignored.

It reminded me of an old computer game called Lemmings. The little characters just kept walking in a straight line until they fell off a cliff. The only way to win was to step in and redirect them. Left alone, they never changed direction on their own.

You can see some version of that in how people behave; where it's easy to keep going in the same direction and stay with whatever is in front of you, especially when it's designed to hold your attention. You can spend a lot of time in something that feels interesting while you are in it and still walk away with nothing.

That is what kept bothering me as I worked through this. If a system can be trained to stop getting pulled into noise and start focusing on what actually leads somewhere, why do people struggle so much to do the same thing for themselves?

I kept thinking about why that happens, and a lot of it comes down to how we operate day to day. Most people fall into patterns without even realizing it. You see something, you respond to it, and before long that becomes your routine. It feels normal because you see it everywhere, and it becomes easy to keep doing the same thing without stopping to ask where it is leading.

There's also something else going on, and it has to do with how we respond to reward. There is a kind of reward that comes from staying occupied, even when nothing is building. You can spend time scrolling, clicking, reacting, and it feels like something is happening. It fills time and makes it feel like you're doing something, even when there is nothing that leads anywhere later.

I think of some classic studies built on the principles of behavioral scientist B. F. Skinner, who studied how rewards shape behavior. In one experiment, hens were placed in front of a touchscreen and learned that pecking a specific image or color led to a reward. They kept pecking as long as something responded, even when the reward itself had no real value beyond that moment. The behavior continued because there was feedback.

In a different way, people do something very similar. We sit in front of our screens, tapping, clicking, searching, waiting for something to feel like progress. It keeps our attention, but it rarely leaves us with anything meaningful.

When I looked at the data from my own research, it was clear that people already have a sense of what gives them meaning. So, the question becomes if you already have some idea of what matters to you, why do you spend so much time doing things that never connect to meaning?

That brings me back to the Noisy TV problem. In the experiment, someone else created a structure that guided that system's attention. In our lives, that structure has often come from outside forces such as school, work, and expectations that have shaped how time is spent. When that structure loosens or disappears, the responsibility shifts in a way many people have never had to deal with directly.

I keep wondering if people are just going to keep walking like the Lemmings in that game and never change direction. Some people will. My hope is if you read this book, you recognize something is missing, and you want more from your life. You can keep doing what you have been doing, or you can pause and choose something different, even if it is a minor adjustment in where you spend your time and attention.

In the game, it only took a small nudge to change direction. For people, those nudges are the decisions you make about what you return to and what you let go of.

That is where adaptive curiosity becomes useful. It helps you pay attention to what possibilities open up and encourages you to stay with them long enough to see where they lead.

At some point, you start to recognize which direction leads somewhere. The real question is whether you follow it.

Appendix

The Meaning Alignment Profile (MAP)

The Meaning Alignment Profile helps you understand **how you naturally experience purpose in everyday life**. It does not measure intelligence, personality, or success. It identifies the kinds of activities that mentally energize you and make your day feel worthwhile.

There are no right or wrong answers.

Answer based on how you typically are, not how you wish you were, or how you think you should respond. Choose the response that best reflects your usual behavior over the past six months.

Work fairly quickly and do not overthink each statement.

Rating Scale

Circle one number for every statement.

1 = Strongly Disagree

2 = Disagree

3 = Neutral/Sometimes True

4 = Agree

5 = Strongly Agree

Do not leave any item blank. If unsure, choose the closest answer.

Section 1 – Exploration

1. I enjoy learning things even when they are not required.
1 2 3 4 5

2. I often look up information simply because I am curious.
1 2 3 4 5

3. I feel energized when I discover something new.
1 2 3 4 5

4. I like understanding how systems or ideas work.
1 2 3 4 5

5. I ask questions even when others seem satisfied with the answer.
1 2 3 4 5

6. I enjoy reading, researching, or studying topics of interest.
1 2 3 4 5

7. I become absorbed in figuring things out.
1 2 3 4 5

8. I am motivated by solving problems or puzzles.
1 2 3 4 5

9. I enjoy intellectual challenges.
1 2 3 4 5

Section 2 – Connection

10. I feel fulfilled when I help someone improve their situation.
1 2 3 4 5

11. I naturally notice when someone needs support or reassurance.
1 2 3 4 5

12. I gain satisfaction from guiding or encouraging others.
1 2 3 4 5

13. I like being someone people can rely on.
1 2 3 4 5

14. I feel good when I make another person's day easier.
1 2 3 4 5

15. I often listen to others' concerns and try to help.
1 2 3 4 5

16. I value meaningful conversations with people.
1 2 3 4 5

17. I feel useful when I can advise or support someone.
1 2 3 4 5

18. I feel motivated when my actions positively affect others.
1 2 3 4 5

Section 3 – Creation

19. I enjoy making or building things.
1 2 3 4 5

20. I like improving or redesigning existing ideas.
1 2 3 4 5

21. I often imagine better ways of doing things.
1 2 3 4 5

22. I feel energized when I start a new project.
1 2 3 4 5

23. I like producing something tangible or visible.
1 2 3 4 5

24. I enjoy creative problem solving.
1 2 3 4 5

25. I am drawn to inventing, designing, or writing.
1 2 3 4 5

26. I prefer creating something new rather than maintaining something old.

1 2 3 4 5

27. I feel satisfied when I complete something I started.

1 2 3 4 5

Section 4 – Influence

28. I naturally take initiative when direction is unclear.

1 2 3 4 5

29. I feel comfortable guiding others toward a goal.

1 2 3 4 5

30. I like organizing people or activities.

1 2 3 4 5

31. I often step forward when decisions need to be made.

1 2 3 4 5

32. I feel responsible for outcomes in group situations.

1 2 3 4 5

33. I prefer directing a project rather than just assisting.

1 2 3 4 5

34. I am motivated when I can shape how something is done.

1 2 3 4 5

35. I like setting plans and helping others follow them.

1 2 3 4 5

36. I feel energized when coordinating efforts toward a shared objective.

1 2 3 4 5

Scoring Your Results

Add the numbers for each section.

Exploration (1–9): ______

Connection (10–18): ______

Creation (19–27): ______

Influence (28–36): ______

Each section ranges from 9 to 45.
Your highest score is your primary pathway.
Your second highest score is your supporting pathway.

Interpreting Your Results

Your results do not tell you what career to choose. They point to the kinds of activities that make your time feel worthwhile, regardless of your role or stage of life. Pay attention to both your highest scores and the sections that felt most accurate as you answered. Those patterns show where your attention naturally goes and where you are more likely to stay engaged.

If your scores are close across multiple sections, that is common. Many people rely on more than one pathway. The goal is not to force a single label, but to understand which pathways consistently impact your behavior.

What Your Scores Mean

HIGH EXPLORATION

You feel purpose when your mind is engaged and learning. This includes a tendency to research topics of interest, read and study, analyze ideas, learn new technologies, solve complex problems, or spend time on strategy games and puzzles. In everyday life, you return to questions even when there is no requirement to do so and you stay with ideas long enough to understand how they work. When this is missing, things can start to feel repetitive or surface level and you may feel like you are moving through routines without much mental engagement. To use this well, choose one area that continues to hold your attention and stay with it long enough to build depth. Treat curiosity as a valid reason to spend your time rather than something that needs justification.

HIGH CONNECTION

You feel purpose when improving another person's experience. This often includes mentoring or tutoring, advising people, coaching individuals, volunteering support, listening and guiding conversations, and helping people navigate decisions. In everyday life, you notice when people need support and tend to step in without being asked, and conversations that go beyond surface-level topics tend to stay with you. When this is missing, interactions can feel transactional and you may feel disconnected even when you are busy. To use this well, be intentional about how you interact by following up on conversations that mattered and creating space for more meaningful exchanges.

HIGH CREATION

You feel purpose when producing or building something. This can include writing, designing, crafting, developing projects, improving systems, building tools or resources, pursuing creative hobbies, or starting personal projects. In everyday life, you feel most engaged when something is taking shape through your effort, and you tend to start ideas or projects and feel satisfied when they move forward. When this is missing, you may feel like your time is being spent without anything to show for it. To use this well, work on something that can develop over time. It does not need to be finished right away. What matters is that you continue working on it long enough to see it take form.

HIGH INFLUENCE

You feel purpose when directing effort and shaping outcomes. This often includes organizing initiatives, planning events, coordinating activities, leading projects, setting goals, and structuring plans for others. In everyday life, you tend to step in when direction is unclear and help organize people or ideas, so things move forward. When this is missing, you may feel underutilized or disconnected from results. To use this well, look for opportunities to contribute your perspective. This does not require a formal role. It begins with offering input when it can help clarify direction.

When Two Scores Are High

EXPLORATION + CREATION

You learn something and then make something with it. In practice, you may collect ideas and then organize them into something tangible. This combination works best when you allow time for both phases so that understanding can turn into output.

EXPLORATION + CONNECTION

You understand and then teach. In practice, you may learn something and then feel the need to discuss it with others or help them understand it through conversation or guidance.

EXPLORATION + INFLUENCE

You analyze and then organize. In practice, you may spend time understanding a situation and then step in to guide how it moves forward, often shaping direction based on what you have learned.

CONNECTION + CREATION

You help people by building solutions for them. In practice, you may notice needs in others and respond by creating something useful such as a guide, a tool, or a resource.

CONNECTION + INFLUENCE

You guide people toward improvement. In practice, you may work closely with people and also help shape their direction through coaching, mentoring, or coordinating group efforts.

CREATION + INFLUENCE

You start and lead projects. In practice, you may begin initiatives and then bring others in to help move them forward, combining building with direction.

When All Four Are Similar

You need variety. A meaningful day includes learning something, helping someone, making something, and organizing something. Without a mix, you may feel restless even when productive.

Common Mistakes When Interpreting Results

Some people answer based on what they think they should value rather than what reflects their actual experience. Others ignore smaller patterns because they do not seem significant, or they wait until they feel completely certain before taking action. This exercise is meant to help you notice patterns, not create a perfect label.

What To Do with This Now

Once you recognize your stronger pathways, begin using that awareness to guide how you spend your time. This does not require a major change. It begins with small decisions about what you explore, how you interact, what you build, and when you step in to contribute. Over time, those choices shape how your days feel. When your actions align with the pathways that naturally engage you, your sense of meaning becomes more consistent. You can return to this section as your experiences change. Your pathways may remain stable, but how you use them will continue to develop.

If you prefer to complete this assessment digitally or revisit it over time, you can access it here: https://meaningalign.netlify.app/. The online version allows you to track your responses and see how your results evolve as your experiences change.

About the Author

Dr. Diane Hamilton is a business behavioral expert, keynote speaker, and Forbes contributor known for her work on curiosity and its impact on innovation, engagement, and performance. She is the creator of the Curiosity Code Index®, a groundbreaking assessment that identifies the barriers to curiosity. Recognized by Thinkers50 Radar as one of the top thinkers in management and leadership, she is a Fulbright Specialist trusted by organizations and audiences around the world. She is the author of *Cracking the Curiosity Code*, *Curiosity Unleashed*, and *The Power of Perception*. Learn more at drdianehamilton.com.

About the Author

Dr. Diane [illegible]

Index